APACHE EXCHANGE

ANN MILLINGTON

Pen Press Publishers Ltd
London

© Ann Millington 1999

All rights reserved

First published in Great Britain by
Pen Press Publishers Ltd
39-41 North Road
London
N7 9DP

ISBN 1 900796 12 0

A catalogue record for this book is available from the
British Library

Front cover: The Trinity
© Fr. John Giuliani
Courtesy of Bridge Building Images Inc.

Cover design by Catrina Sherlock

This book is dedicated to Youth Services all over the world. The work they do with young people - the ignored, misunderstood, blamed and criticised but desperately needy part of society - is of immeasurable worth. For upon these youthful shoulders the future of tomorrow's world will rest.

Acknowledgements

Thanks are extended to Fr.Bernard Green and Sr.Darlene Pienschke for their enthusiasm and help with research into the Sunrise Ceremony; to Fr.Ed Fronske for insights into real Apacheland and to the Arizona Historical Society for the background history of the region and details of Fort Apache.

The support of so many people, in so many different ways, in North Staffordshire and Arizona, is very much appreciated - they all gave over and above what was expected. The effect was humbling and heart-warming.

Special thanks go to Birmingham Catholic Youth Service and Karen Kent for roping us in and getting us involved; and with great sincerity to the West Midlands Youth Exchange Committe - without their funding it would all have been just an impossible dream.

The Returners were:-

Catherine Talbot	Catherine Hill	Rachel Powell
Frances Matthews	Paul Wright	William Dawes
Stephen Wheatley	Chris Scott	Aidan Pepper
Ann Millington	Kath Ryan	Fr.David Newell

Preface

We all have our own mental picture of Red Indians, mostly, or even entirely, drawn from Western films or popular fiction. In more sympathetic portrayals they are seen as silent, inscrutable, noble savages. But mostly, they are the villains - drunken, cruel and vengeful men, living in primitive dwellings with subservient squaws; worthless, lazy, good-for-nothings - impossible to civilise. This is the picture we have been handed of a hundred and fifty years ago and has inspired many people to want to know more about them and discover if what we have been told is really true.

Although we know now that they are more correctly called Native Americans and are slowly beginning to realise they possess knowledge superior to ours in some areas, the stereotype war-whooping, war-painted, tomahawk wielding in'jun warrior is the image that springs most readily to mind. But what is it really like today?

The purpose of this book is to record a particularly significant exchange that brought together Apache and English youngsters to experience something of each other's lifestyles. The whole enterprise grew, as do so many brilliant ideas, from a chance remark. Remarks are ten a penny - but in the right place at the right time and into the receptive ears of someone who can make things happen, that chance remark becomes a springboard for action.

Fr. Bernard Green, Salvatorian missionary to the Cibecue Apache in Arizona, returns, whenever possible, to his home in Stoke on Trent, Staffordshire, visiting his mother and maintaining his contact with St. Teresa's parish. When he happened to say how much the Apaches questioned him about England and that they have some very funny ideas about us, the Trent Vale parishioners quickly seized on the idea of bringing some over here for a visit. The main problem, of course, was finance; some serious fundraising would be a necessity.

Here was another stroke of luck. Karen Kent, Staffordshire Area Youth Officer for the Birmingham Catholic Youth Service was a St. Teresa's parishioner and offered the Youth Service's help and enthusiasm. The idea snowballed into a youth project. A successful application was made to the West Midlands Youth Exchange Committee for a travel subsidy and in no time the visit of the Apaches had become a two-way cultural exchange, funded by the European Union, through the British Council. The Youth Exchange is an initiative to promote inter-racial understanding between young people, primarily within Europe, but extending now to other parts of the world.

What was planned was an incoming visit by the White Mountain Apaches in October 1996 and a return visit by young Staffordians in July 1997.

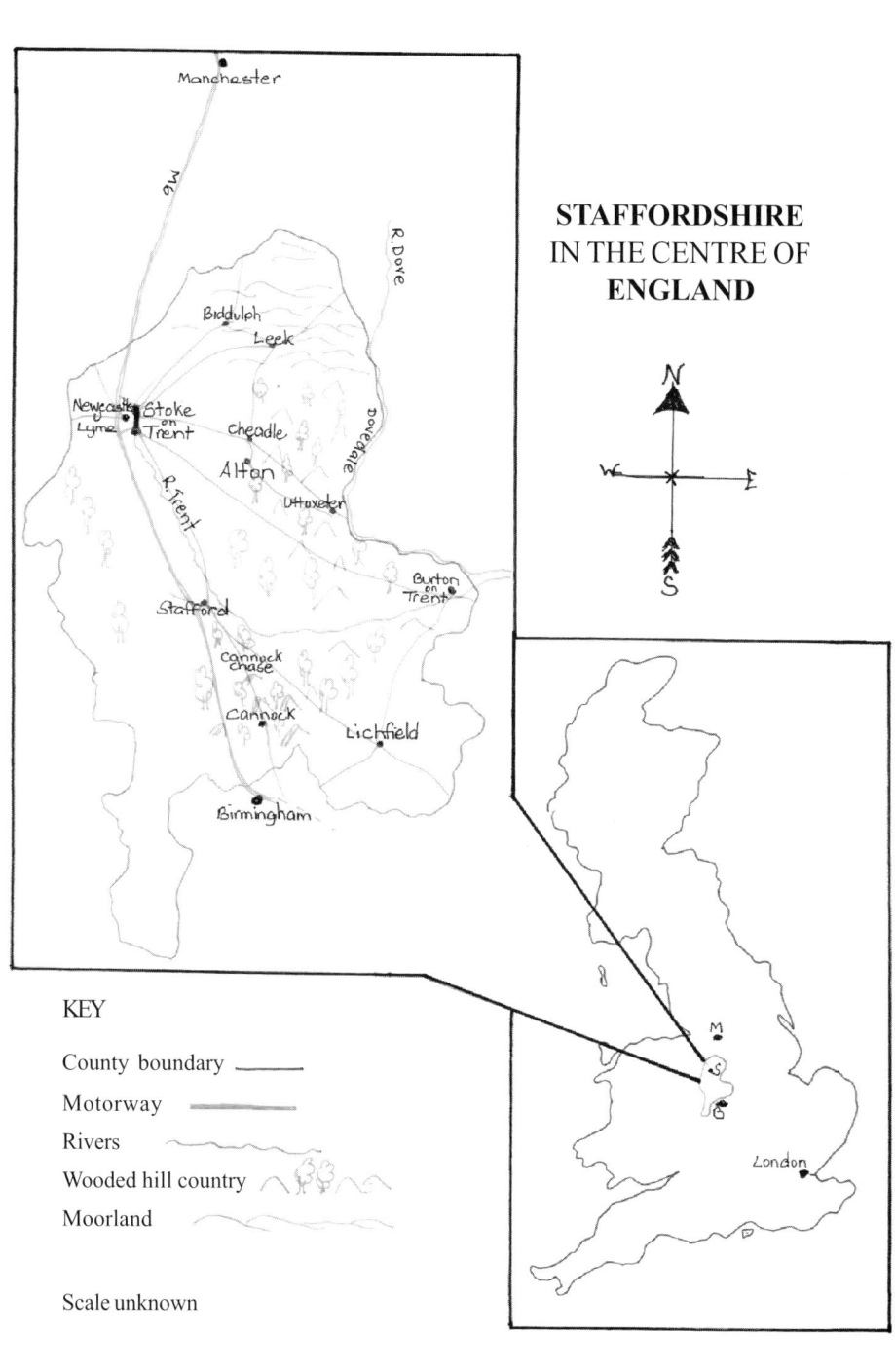

From Arizona To Staffordshire

The decision to undertake a major Apache adventure had been made; the next step was to gather together a group of suitably aged youths that were keen to go and able to raise the necessary funds. This was not easy. Five adults, who would be able to contribute themselves, although not qualifying for the exchange grant, eventually enlarged the group of seven to twelve. The parishes of Staffordshire would fund the accommodation, transport and food, once the Apaches arrived, but the fares still presented an almost impossible obstacle. Fr. Bernard's parishioners began a year of intensive fundraising.

The first effort was a basketball tournament at the High School, but before this could take place, forest fires in the area meant that the High School gymnasium was taken over by the firefighters and the tournament was postponed. As with many postponed events, the initial impetus was missing, some teams had pulled out, some referees did not turn up and disagreements flared between team members. However some money was made eventually. Happily, an American parish, one of many that support the American Missions, donated a car to be sold and this was a big help. Sales of clothing contributed something and a community dance brought in a small amount. Enough was collected to set the party on its way.

How far can you go, today, without paperwork? Not very far! Native Americans, not being world travellers, face, it seems, special problems in getting passports. Tribal identity does not appear to be adequate. Who has a birth certificate? Where can it be? Department of Transport identification and three signed affidavits agreeing you are who you say you are, can set you on the way to

Above: Apache group with hosts
Below: Sr Daralene & Fr Bernard

Phoenix for a day of office searching, form filling, document presenting and of course - the inevitable waiting. This was the quest of many of the group and did eventually produce the all-important passports, although at least one would-be traveller was disappointed and had to be left behind.

At last, seven young people and five adults with Fr. Bernard and Sister Darlene Pienschke landed early on Wednesday, October 2nd 1996 at Manchester Airport and were whisked away down the M6 into deepest Staffordshire, to begin their part of the exchange. There was Janell from Whiteriver, Deanna from Cibecue and El Maria, from Mesa; the boys, all from Whiteriver, were Janell's brother, Reagan, Darren and brothers Frank and Armadio. They were all aged between 15 and 20. The Apache adults were Darren's mother, Margaret, Rose and her daughter, Lee Ann and Theresa all from Whiteriver and Juanita from Cibecue. They were all dressed for travelling in jeans, tee shirts and warm jackets - but they were unmistakably Native American in their facial features, their long, raven-black hair, worn either loose or plaited.

It was not a kind October, certainly not kind to Apaches used to Arizona's fierce conditions. It was grey, it was rainy and it was unusually windy; although there were still leaves on the trees and an abundance of grass underfoot, there was also an abundance of mud and wild, cool days.

If the climate was so different, then what could be said about the accommodation? The Archdiocese of Birmingham is fortunate to own Alton Castle, which up to recently had been a boarding school and is now run as a Youth Facility. This provided a home for the travellers for most of their two week stay and what a home!

To most people, a castle is a romantic place, stirring thoughts of olden days, of knights riding out; of lords and ladies; fortresses against marauding enemies; vast buildings of stone, their walls soaring to battlements, their iron-studded, oaken doors steadfast against those who would break in, protective to those sheltering inside. Alton Castle fulfils this picture, perched, as it is on a rock precipice, towering over the village of Alton in the scenic countryside of the Weaver Hills, known to so many who visit the

Above: Stone battlements, towers and chimneys - Alton Castle
Below: Looking over the coutryside - the castle above the trees

nearby Alton Towers. Inside it is surprisingly cosy. The high-ceilinged rooms have ornate open fire places; mullioned windows look out on spectacular views; twisty spiral stone stairs lead upwards to graceful turrets or downwards to comfortable kitchens - stone walls and central heating.

The normal work of the Castle - residential courses for school groups of primary school children - continued while the Apache visitors settled into their more private community rooms of a dormitory for the boys and more spacious, shared rooms for the girls. A living room with cooking facilities provided a good place to relax and be themselves, getting away for a while from all the unfamiliar attention they would receive in the next two weeks. The castle minibus stood outside waiting to transport them wherever the packed schedule required, meeting so many people and seeing so many unimagined things.

How intriguing was the sight of the milkman, delivering early morning milk to the households of Alton. "How ever does he know who wants what?" they puzzled, as the milkfloat trundled round the village, stopping for the milkman to deposit bottles of milk on the doorsteps.

As hosts, we wished to be very welcoming, to show how much we wanted them, and how much we were prepared to make their stay here enjoyable. We wanted them to like us and to understand that we liked them and then to expand this feeling into things much bigger than just a holiday visit. Whereas most of the facilitating - car driving, food providing and contact making - was, of necessity, handled by adults, the eight teenage hosts were there at every possible occasion breaking down the barriers of distance and culture, weaving a new set-up as only the young can.

There was so much to show about the life of ordinary people in England and perhaps the most important was that we don't actually live in castles! One Sunday, the party was shared out among the hosts and entertained in their homes for a traditional Sunday lunch and a chance to meet their hosts' extended families.

North Staffordshire is world famous for the pottery industry, so it was inevitable that a tour was arranged of the Wedgwood

*Above: Outside the Gladstone Pottery Museum
Below: Making china flowers*

Apache Exchange

factory, but first a visit to the Gladstone Pottery Museum which puts a different perspective on the ware we all take for granted. This museum is a restored working "pot bank"; working in the way potting was carried on before the electrification of the kilns and mechanisation. Here the craft processes are explained, the old engines worked, and visitors can walk inside the old bottle ovens to see how ware was stacked inside for firing. Anyone can try their hand at the traditional skills and those who tried china flower making eventually had something to take home with them. The work in the olden days was very labour-intensive and very arduous; the conditions were poor, the hours long and the wages low; homes huddled around the great smoking, coal-fired kilns - bad conditions still within living memory. Much has changed since those days, but not everything. At the ultra-modern Wedgwood factory, the old skills of the potter are still highlighted; people from the workbench take turns to go into the visitor centre to demonstrate that, although modern methods of mass production have taken over from the old, it is still a very artistic and skilful craft. That so large a workforce possesses this creative talent is quite remarkable on its own. All around the visitor centre are displays of famous Wedgwood china, fantastic designs, decorated and gilded so that it looks like a treasure cave.

Near to Alton is the premier JCB factory, where the amazing earthmovers are made, so a tour of this was in programme. One of the surprising things was that this factory, like Wedgwood, is set in the countryside, making it more pleasant for the workers, among other reasons; a stark contrast to the image of the industrial midlands held by so many people.

On the first Saturday, a group of students from St. Margaret Ward High School, took the whole party of Apaches to Dovedale, in the Peak District National Park, to sample a particularly beautiful part of our county and next-door Derbyshire. This day was the only dry and sunny day of the Apache's visit and we hoped it would be something a bit like home to them, being wild and natural. They had been surprised that everywhere they had been, had been under concrete or tarmac and that the houses were so many and so close

Above: Outside Ilam Hall - Dovedale
Below: The Mayor of Stafford joined in the Hoop Dance

together; everywhere so tidy and orderly - but the countryside was so green, so very, very green. We surprised them again during the trek along the banks of the River Dove when one of them was stung by stinging nettles. Immediately dock leaves were found to rub on the sting and soothe the hurt. They had not expected us to use such old, natural cures in this day and age of science; but of course, we, too have our race memory, ancient lore, retained long after current technology needs to be updated.

The minibus worked overtime, transporting the party around this scenic and predominantly agricultural county, but with its significant industrial conurbation of North Staffordshire. Half a million people live and work in the northern third of the county; a quarter of a million live in the 12 miles long and 3 miles wide, City of Stoke-on-Trent which follows the infant River Trent in its narrow upper valley. This density of population is so different from the Apache environment in Arizona.

Shopping trips to Hanley were very popular, as of course, was the day at nearby Alton Towers. One evening some of the young ones went to the New Victoria Theatre in Newcastle-under-Lyme to see a modern production of Romeo and Juliet, as they were studying it for their exams. Two of the most culture-binding topics were school subjects and pop music - which was just as it should be in a Youth Exchange.

However, meeting people was to be the major thrust of the exchange and it says much for the resilience of the Apache that they were not totally overwhelmed by the attention they received. There was a grand reception for our Sponsors, held on first Thursday evening in the castle. Fr. Bernard explained something of the Apache culture; the ladies danced the hoop dance; Margaret sang in Apache and then English a beautiful song called *"I Walk In Beauty"*, accompanying herself on the pot drum. Then there was a speech of welcome from Lord Stafford and an exchange of gifts. The Apaches had brought representations of their Great Seal while we presented them all with special Apache Exchange tee shirts and sweatshirts. There was also a celebration cake, made by Kath Ryan, ceremonially cut by Lord Stafford and Teresa.

*Above: Rose presents the Great Seal to Lord Stafford
Below: Margaret sang in Apache and English*

Apache Exchange

Being a cultural exchange between the Catholic parishes of Cibecue, Cedar Creek and Whiteriver and the Staffordshire area of the Catholic Archdiocese of Birmingham, naturally there was a lot of contact with the schools. Interested Catholic schools had been activated to research Native Americans. As their contribution to the exchange, they worked to stock the castle with food for the visit, sending decorated "breakfast boxes" which overflowed with every imaginable comestible and which long outlasted the visit.

One morning, the Year 6 of each school gathered in the castle's gym to meet the Apaches, ask their many questions, listen to the descriptions of Apache life and to dance, Apache-style, the Rabbit Dance. However, in spite of all that had been said before the Apaches came, they still expected bows and arrows and feathers and were very pleasantly surprised at how kind and friendly they really are. The Apache boys at this gathering wore their everyday jeans, tee shirts and trainers, for there does not seem to be any traditional dress for men, but the girls and women wore their traditional "Camp Dress". This consists of a long, full and tiered skirt with a matching top in colourful cotton, unmistakeably trimmed and decorated. Soft buckskin boots, with turned up toes and exquisite, Apache turquoise and multicoloured beaded necklaces, bracelets and rings completed the picture. Lee Ann showed the children typical Apache articles like the "burden basket" - a general purpose carrying basket woven from yucca fibres, conical in shape, trimmed with tin jingles, which fits so comfortably over one shoulder. There was a "dream catcher" - like a spider's web, made from thongs, which is put near a child's bed to catch the dreams that come in through the windows at night. The good dreams slip thought the web but the bad dreams get caught and, as the sun comes up, they melt away in its heat. She showed a "cradle board" into which newborn babies are put, tightly bound so they do not fall out. They can be carried around without being mauled and put down in safety, feeling secure. It is said that the hardness of the cradle board makes the baby grow with a strong straight back and that many babies are reluctant to leave their cradle boards even when they become too heavy to carry about.

Above Left: LeeAnn shows a burden basket
Above Right: Rose demonstrates a cradleboard
Below: Leading the Rabbit Dance with the Year 6s

"Why don't the boys have a special dress?" the children wanted to know.

"They just don't," was the answer. "They just wear cowboy clothes and very smart cowboy clothes for special occasions."

"And why don't they wear feathers?"

Feathers are not everyday wear. They are very special, sacred things, the children were told. Eagle feathers are the most holy because the eagle, flying so high, is very near the Great Spirit, God, and close to His thoughts. They are found when the eagle moults them; no one kills eagles for their feathers and they are often difficult to find, so they are greatly valued. Feathers are used for sacred ceremonies and for serious events. They can only be worn by someone who is worthy. In some places, where there are no eagle feathers, the feathers of other birds are acceptable - like the turkey. Turkeys do not fly high, but the Great Spirit recognises them as having a special honour among the people as they have provided food for many thousands of years. Feathers, or the lack of them, excited people of all ages who met the Apaches; it was the one thing that sprang to mind at the mention of the word "Apache". Fr. Bernard had a unique opportunity to link all the misconceptions of both cultures and wearing his exotic, decorated shirt, jeans and cowboy hat, addressed many audiences, putting the facts right.

The very early settlers doubted the humanity of the native peoples they met, at first. It caused great suspicion, seeing them so adept at living without the amenities of "civilisation"; living entirely on the natural things around them like the animals in the forests, while they, the newcomers, struggled to merely exist in the New World. The totally different values of the two peoples brought conflict and then later, the insatiable demand for land and the exploitation for financial gain versus the resistance of the Native Americans to this threat to their way of life, bred ambition, fear, trickery, revenge and war. In the Indian Wars, the winner, the US Government, took all and the loser, scorned and despised, became a problem which has occupied, in varying degrees, an entire government department ever since. Native Americans became "non-persons" in the land that they were part of and a concentrated process began to remove any feeling or knowledge of their true identity; this process went on until the 1960s, when at last the authorities discontinued the policy.

Today's Apache and the other Native American Tribes, are struggling to establish themselves as valid nations in the United States; to live in this modern world, with all its technology and yet remain faithful to the traditions that have sustained them for thousands of years. Yet it is so difficult to repair the damage of the last hundred and fifty years; the self-esteem of the Apache is very low and under the government regulations, no help is given to raise expectations and kick-start an economy. Reserva-tion Apache pay no taxes and therefore receive no benefits. Life is hard, work is scarce, despair is rife and desperation drives many into the spiral of drink, drugs and suicide. Slowly the situation is changing due to the organised determination of the Tribal Council, aided by voluntary Anglo agencies, who teach in the schools, work in the hospital, help set up commercial enterprises and minister in the various churches.

This is what Fr. Bernard and Sr. Darlene explained to the audiences that they met as they travelled around the county; while the Apaches demonstrated aspects of their lives in their own quiet way and patiently answered the multitude of questions.

People came from all over the county for the Apache Mass. It was held at St. Teresa's and was just the ordinary Sunday mass, but with a difference. The crowded church echoed to the sound of the drum as the Apaches danced their way in, jingles jingling. There was sacred smoke, and sacred pollen for blessings and long Apache prayer chants. Taking the Offertory collection had a new dimension when a burden basket travelled through the congregation, into which people symbolically placed their worries and troubles, their thanks and successes as part of their offering to God. All the familiar liturgy was there, at that Mass, but something extra, as well, that touched a special place. This union of two traditions in the Christian family will long be remembered by all those who were part of it; as will the wonderful hospitality of Trent Vale parish at the buffet lunch.

So the incoming leg proceeded, surprise piled on surprise for both parties who had known about each other only through films, television and books. Nothing works better than personal contact. The touch of warm hand on warm hand, eye to eye, smile to smile created a bond that stretched four thousand miles.

"The people would look at us with such respect and admiration," said Deanna. "I felt as though I was something special instead of just an Apache, ignored on a reservation."

"I didn't know anything about them, before they came," confessed one of the hosts. "I understand so much more now."

Tears were shed as the visitors loaded the minibus and prepared to leave the castle on the first stage of their journey home. Crowds were there to wish them God speed. There had been a farewell Mass at Alton, followed by a meal, for all who cared to brave a particularly wet Sunday afternoon drive along the miles of twisty country roads to the castle - twice as many people arrived than had been realistically expected; so profound had been the impact on our whole community of this unique visit. The deeply spiritual atmosphere of the Mass, the polite, good humoured sharing of the meal and the sentiments expressed to the departing guests, that gloomy October evening, produced a tingle in the air that sizzled; no one, who was there, will ever forget it.

It took some time to sort the turmoil of information and impression left in our minds after those two hectic weeks, to rearrange our personal picture of "Apache". Now we knew so much more, we knew individuals with names, we knew their voices, had heard them laugh. We took them into our lives; we added them to our own personal lists of concerns. A link had been forged, anchored firmly in Staffordshire; the next step was to attend to the other end, in faraway Arizona.

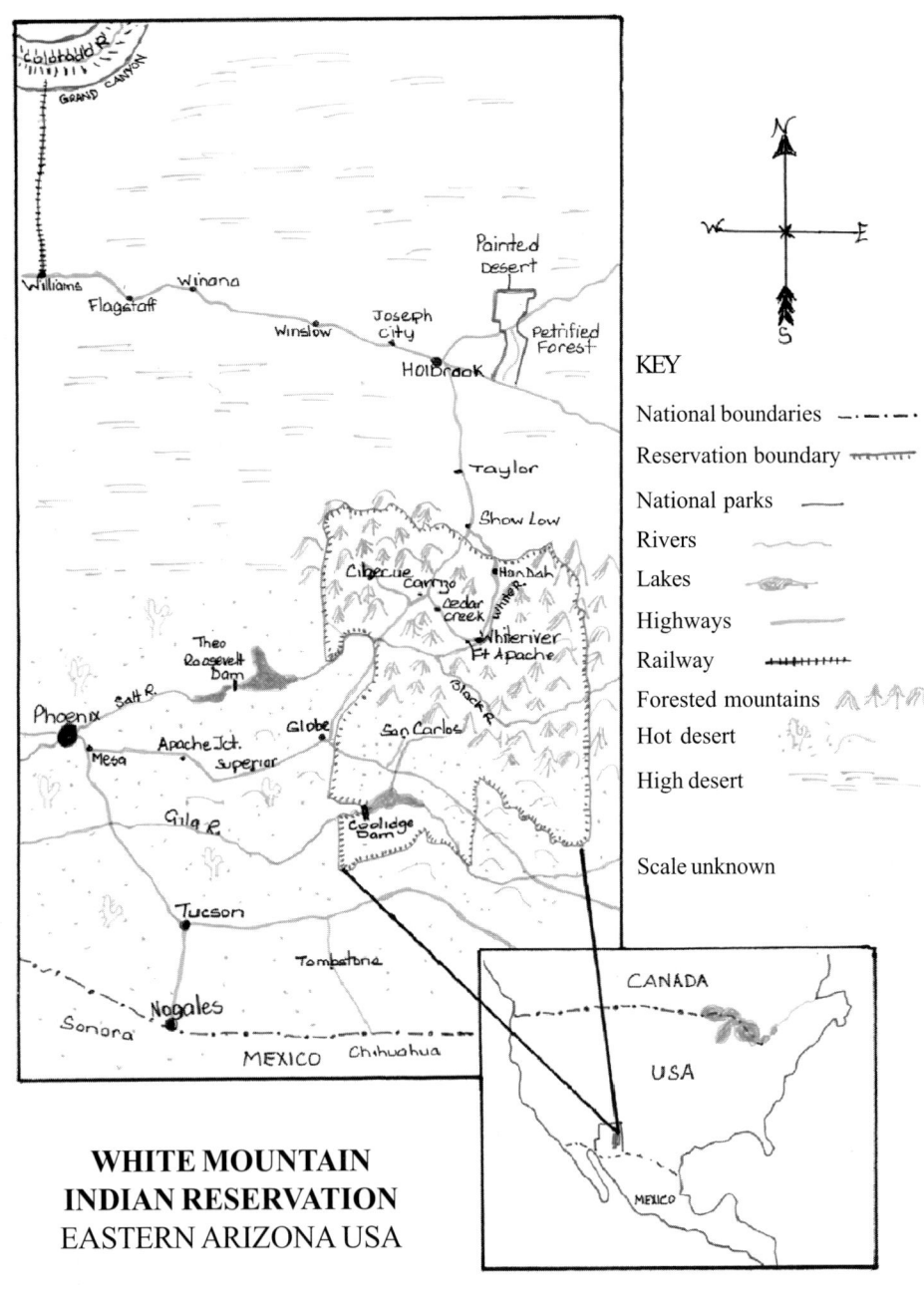

**WHITE MOUNTAIN INDIAN RESERVATION
EASTERN ARIZONA USA**

From Staffordshire To Arizona

New Year 1997 - it was time to start thinking about the return visit. There was the added complication that Karen had a career-move and in a few weeks would be out of the picture. Karen, who had masterminded the incoming leg and should have seen the project through in sunny Arizona, would be away in another dimension, with other things on her mind, at the crucial time. The reins were handed to me as a Youth Leader and Native American enthusiast. I had been involved in the incoming leg, visiting primary schools to talk about the visit, helping with catering, transporting and fundraising. To the question, "Would you be prepared to take the return leg to Arizona?" I immediately replied, "Yes!"

It was only later that I thought, "What have I done!" What was I thinking of? A retired teacher, grandmother of two, cavorting about America with a gang of teenagers! But although the outside of me is a retired grandmother, the inside of me is not. It has still the reckless instincts of youth and a willingness to have a go at any challenge - tempered, of course with the wisdom of maturity...but not too much. So I joined a fitness club to get the outside me in shape for what would probably be a taxing two weeks and set about the organisation and administration of a lifetime dream.

Kath Ryan also jumped at the chance to go. She was another of the willing hands behind the scenes of the incoming leg, working quietly at whatever needed to be done and very interested in Native American culture. Neither of us thought, when the Apaches were here, that we stood any chance at all of going to Arizona; we were too far down the list of candidates. Kath is an RGN - Registered General Nurse - and what a good qualification that is for getting you into places where others fear to tread! She began to assemble the medical supplies we might need. Such is her dread of snakes, anti-venom was at the top of the list - but we never saw a single live snake the whole time we were there. She lives in Birmingham and therefore nearer to the Youth Service's bank account, she became the group's Treasurer, immediately setting about finding the best deal to get us to Apacheland.

That was the girls' chaperones sorted, but finding someone for the boys proved more difficult. Although when two weeks living on an Apache reservation was mentioned, nearly everyone said eagerly, "Can I come to carry your bags?" when it came to actually volunteering to come along - no one! He had to have some qualification in working with young people so we were looking for a youth worker or priest - willing, available, physically able to stand up to the rigours of the unknown and able to contribute to the spiritual dimension of the exchange - and preferably residing in Staffordshire. None of the youth workers in the county was available at the end of July, so we moved onto the list of suitable priests. Like policemen, you can never find a priest when you need one, but diligence paid off. After a sales pitch that only the most dismal and unimaginative could refuse, Fr. David Newell joined the team. The Leadership was a triumvirate.

Letters with the outline details of the return visit had been sent to all the Catholic Secondary Schools in the county and to all the parishes with an invitation to young, interested people to make an application. It was oversubscribed. It was undersubscribed. People opted in and then dropped out, we waited in vain to hear from those who said they might; but by Easter the Return team was established - three leaders and eight youngsters. Again the youngest was 15 and the oldest twenty. Stephen and Will had been hosts at the castle and already knew each other, Paul comes from Burntwood in the south of the county and Chris, man of the world and experienced chef, comes from St. Teresa's parish. Of the girls, Fran had been a host and Catherine T had been on the Dovedale expedition, they knew Stephen and Will, slightly, while Catherine H, also from Burntwood, only knew Paul. Rachel only knew Chris because she is from St. Teresa's too. Meetings with parents took place and one Saturday, Fr. David held a get together for the team and their parents and serious plans were made for raising funds. There would be personal sponsorship, where an individual's finances were boosted by their own efforts and joint sponsorship, where we all worked together to raise a significant sum which we would share. The bric-a-brac stall at Newcastle Carnival, the sale of key-rings and tee shirts, the sponsored Fitness Challenge at Esporta Health Club, the Pie and Peas Supper not only raised £1400 but also served to bond the group. It must be said however, that we never, ever managed to have the whole group together in one place at one time. Donations came in from the Lions Clubs, from some schools and parishes and community clubs, which were gratefully received with promises to recount our adventures to them when we returned. The Grant from the Youth Exchange Committee arrived, without this the exchange could not even have been contemplated and, of course, the parents made up the difference - the Return was on track.

One Sunday afternoon was devoted to sorting out what we were actually going to do, when we got there. We had a programme of activities arranged by Fr. Bernard and Sr. Darlene, so they could show us Apacheland, as we had shown Staffordshire to them, but we needed something of our culture to share. The Apache contribution to the Mass had impressed everyone here, so we decided to be able to put an English contribution into the Mass over there; we diligently rehearsed the responses and four songs, some which we found in a hymn book they left behind and some that we were particularly fond of ourselves. We could also sing The Lord's Prayer in a modern setting; in fact everything was so up to date we had to discover the procedure for taking a guitar with us. It was at this meeting that Aidan joined the return group, the twelfth place was filled, and filled by a musician.

There were two Final Meetings because we still could not get everyone together at one time, even when the group was featured at the Christian Arts Festival, "Emmaus '97", two days before departure, there were two or three members who didn't make it.

So it was a relief when, at last, all the Apache Returners assembled at Birmingham Airport at eight o'clock in the morning, on Tuesday July 22nd - with guitar, camcorder, a generous supply of sunscreen lotion and a baseball cap each, donated by American Airlines, added to all the usual luggage of the intrepid traveller.

We did not know each other well at all. Five of us had met at other youth events but contact for the majority had been confined to the rather disjointed preparations, so twelve individuals were launched westwards, each with their own particular idea of what was in store. Some thought it would be an interesting holiday; some liked the idea of meeting up with Apache friends they had met in October; some were keen on anything to do with Native Americans; none knew what to expect other than it would be very, very hot. All, however, were deeply sincere Christians, strong in their Faith, ready to experience whatever new situations had to offer and not shy to make a contribution of their own. The great adventure had begun and the Atlantic Ocean slipped away below.

Seven and a half hours later, after flying over Canada and Lake Michigan, we landed at Chicago's O'Hare Airport with a comfortable time to discover where to find the plane for Phoenix and where we too were discovered. Fr. David's distant cousin, Mary, who had heard we were coming through Chicago, met us at the departure gate and presented us each with stylish Chicago Bulls baseball caps. This brief, but heartwarming encounter seemed to set a seal on the whole enterprise; that someone should take the trouble to travel out to the airport; to find out where we would depart from; bring gifts, thoughtfully appropriate for youngsters; in order to wish us well during our stay in America, gave us a glow. We would have liked to stay longer. But onwards we went, south-west from Chicago, across the continent, over farmlands, rivers, and over mountains until, dropping down, the land flattened out first in varieties of sandy colours then startling green rectangles laid out like a gigantic chequer-board, we had arrived at Phoenix on the edge of the Gila Desert. Of course the first thing was to locate our luggage which was surprisingly easy and, at the very first glance round, there was Fr. Bernard and Sr. Darlene and, yes,

Janell and her mother, holding a banner "Welcome Brits to Apacheland". Such hugs and greetings, so many photographs and video footage, then out, out into Arizona.

Was it hot? It was like opening an oven door; the heat nearly knocked you off you feet. It was 36.6C (98F) on the thermometer, in the shade and it was now 5pm! Thank goodness we had plenty of sunscreen lotion for our blond, blue-eyed, fair skinned party. It says a lot for our sun protection that no-one returned home sunburnt. Fr. Bernard brought a smart minibus round to our waiting spot and Reagan Armstrong Sr. loaded our luggage into his pick-up; the last 200-mile stage of our journey began.

The concrete road out of Phoenix was straight; the houses along the road were made from sandy or red coloured stone; they seemed either quite exotic in their architecture or low-rise, high-density developments in a sort of Mexican style. Growing here and there were palm trees of various sizes and several varieties of cactus and other such vegetation, none of which looked very permanent or happy and no weeds. The road was straight, we drove on and on and the habitations became fewer and fewer. The dry sandiness, punctuated by tall Saguaro cactus, gave way to sparse grass and little bushes, which, as we were climbing steadily but slowly, became more abundant - but not much. The land seemed flat, but dramatic hills of sun-mellowed sandstone reared into view and receded as we swept past. The sun set in a blaze of fiery glory and we were definitely climbing up into the mountains and pretty spectacular ones at that. However, when the sun set, the twilight was very short and with the darkness we immediately fell into disturbed and fitful sleep.

The lights of Whiteriver stirred us and soon the minibus stopped outside St. Francis' Retreat Centre - it was only 8.30pm Arizona time but we had been journeying for 26 hours and the dead, cold desperation of fatigue overcame us as we were shown where everything was and how things worked. Then Fr. Bernard and Sr. Darlene left us to drive the 60 miles back to their homes in Cibecue with the instructions to use the next day to recover from our jet lag and be ready, in the evening, to go to a cookout.

Above: Welcome! Hon Dah!
Below: St Francis' Church, Whiteriver

The boys had already made a thorough investigation of the kitchen, eaten a big bag of crisps and made cups of tea all round. This revived us quite well and as we were still waiting for our luggage to arrive, we sorted out our sleeping arrangements.

The Retreat Centre is a facility for visiting groups to stay in Whiteriver for a variety of religious and community events and is entirely self-sufficient and air-conditioned. The community room with dining table at one end, two settees and other home comforts, including TV, is the largest room. Off this is the kitchen with a well-filled fridge-freezer, large gas cooker and cupboards stocked with dry goods and all you could wish in utensils. Leading from the community room, a corridor runs down to a door at the other end of the building. Off the corridor, on the left, is a laundry room complete with washer, dryer and ironing facilities, then two bedrooms and a bathroom, which were taken over by the girls. On the right side are two more bedrooms and a bathroom, which were for the boys. The bedrooms were just about big enough for one untidy person or two tidy ones - we sorted out the space for twelve of us. For the girls - no problem. Rachel and Fran had the double bed and Catherine T had a camp bed in one room, while Catherine H had a camp bed in the other girl's room with Kath and me, we had a single bed each - in deference to our old age. Readily identifying the Catherines was never really solved. The two Catherines did not shorten their names and anyway we already had a Kath. Neither had a nickname, they were both of about the same height and build and both had long blond hair, both were musical. The only difference between them, we ultimately discovered, is that Catherine H is a world authority on Star Trek and Catherine T isn't, so for the whole time we first had to establish to which Catherine we were referring.

The boys presented a problem which our exhausted minds grappled with for many a while and were the occasion of somewhat ribald humour. In one bedroom there was a double bed and in the other, a double bed and a camp bed. It was easy to establish that Fr. David should have the bed-settee in the community room but all five boys wanted to be the one who had the camp bed, none of

Above: Beautiful Apacheland
Below: Testing the sun - the Retreat Centre

them was willing to share. The machinations, the permutations, the tossing of coins, the careful reasonings were of no avail and by the time the luggage arrived we were all far too tired to care anyway. So those who knew where they were sleeping left them to it and, in no time at all, the silence of sleep descended on St. Francis' Retreat Centre. It had been Will's 17th birthday and he had had two days worth of a day.

We woke relatively early to what was literally a new world, a world totally different from the one we had left so far behind. In spite of knowing we were going to the White Mountains, we had omitted to think about actual mountains - our thoughts concentrated on hot desert. We had never really appreciated that we were in the mountains; that we were surrounded by mountains and forests; that the sky could possibly be so blue; the sun so golden and the air so sweet - and we were in the middle of the town of Whiteriver. Now, some of us are early-morning people and some of us definitely are not. All early morning people know that this is a very special time of day, everywhere in the world. There is magic in the air as the sun warms up the rousing earth and we, who leapt out of bed at the crack of dawn, saw humming birds sipping at scarlet gladioli and dragonflies skimming the dusty car park. We could sit on the doorstep with a cup of tea and piece of toast and quietly talk about serious things until the sleepyheads emerged. Sitting on the doorstep, with a coke or tea or water, was a good place to be, at any time; observing the world and even watching the eagle soaring overhead, on his way heavenwards.

All the buildings in Whiteriver, indeed in all Apacheland, hug the ground. There are no skyscrapers here. Modest homes of one storey are scattered in the town, each with plots of land for parking pick-up trucks, grazing horses and minimal gardening. The highway seems to be the only hard road and it travels straight through the reservation with only a few side roads, most of which are dirt tracks. Fences are pretty low key too, so there is a feeling of spaciousness and freedom. This is not to say that there are no significant buildings in Whiteriver, it is after all, the administration centre for the White Mountain Apache and has the usual amenities of a town, including lighting along the highway. The Tribal Centre is a brick building; the High School is typical; the supermarkets are recognisable in the style we all know; there are several churches of varying denominations and there are the inevitable filling stations for the many cars and pick-ups. Judging by the car park at the Tribal Centre, sizeable crowds are expected at times, although at the 1990 census Apaches numbered around 18,000, but not all living on the reservation. The people we saw seemed very purposeful, but you could hardly say Whiteriver was fired up with activity.

When all the Returners were up and about, the first priority was to phone home to tell the parents that we had arrived safely. With great forethought we had arranged that one set of parents would receive the call and then cascade the information, in a chain to the rest, thereby saving on transatlantic charges and it fell to Paul to start the chain off - 10am Arizona time, 6pm at home. Then it was decided that a shopping expedition was needed to obtain more fresh milk, bread and water. Yes, there was water in the taps which we were assured was drinkable - except it was a bit cloudy, like when the water boards have been disturbing the pipes at home. Anyway, we needed the containers for carrying water with us when we were out and about. Needless to say, when we had no bottled water, we all drank the tap water very thankfully. In fact we drank more water, that fortnight, that we would ever drink in a comparable time, in the rest of our lives!

The boys had already been exploring and knew where the supermarket, "Basha's", was, so they and Kath, armed with the traveller's cheques, set off to shop, while the girls tested the sun and we sorted out what was already feeling like home.

It was two miles to the supermarket and it was already quite hot. The shoppers had found a lot more "necessities" - like ice cream, popcorn and a polystyrene cool-box, which meant that they borrowed a shopping trolley to carry them the two miles home. Paul and Will volunteered to return it while Chris, Steve and Aidan promised to provide a magnificent brunch for us all, when they got back.

It had not gone unnoticed by the leadership, that the boys were taking on all the chores, while the girls sat back and let them, so to even things out, a rota was drawn up where everyone, including the leaders, took an equal share in communal tasks.

Time seemed to go very slowly, that day - we even managed two loads of washing, pegging it out on the washing line at the back. We also took delivery of clothing donated to the parish by a passer-by. At last we were able to meet our hosts and become acquainted with the day-to-day life of St. Francis' Mission. The priest of Whiteriver is Fr. Ed Fronske OFM and his parish stretches from the northern boundary of the reservation to Cedar Creek where it meets Fr. Bernard's parish. Helping him in Whiteriver are Brother Ernie LuVisi OFM and Sister Mary Hottenroth SBS, but even though we stayed with them for nearly two weeks, we did not actually see very much of them; they were kept very busy in their parish work.

We could not resist looking inside the church of St. Francis where we would focus some of our activities in the coming days. From the outside, St. Francis' looks just like the Spanish mission churches seen in films, although this building is only about 75 years old. Inside, the coolness and quietness is tangible and there is a happy mixture of traditional Apache and traditional European decor. The old high altar, at the eastern end of the church, ornate and conventional, flanked by statues is, nevertheless enhanced by a display of feathers and backed by a triptych of the Passion, Crucifixion and Resurrection. However the altar that is used today is situated halfway down the church, beside the right hand wall, facing the congregation. The action of the Mass is right among the people. This altar is plainer, with an Apache seal painted on the front and an altar cloth of ethnic pattern laid on top. Behind the altar, a mural of the Franciscan crucifix blends into an Apache wickiup frame, flanked by the Crown Dancers, while above all, arches the rainbow - a symbol of hope recognised the world over. Around the walls are the conventional Stations of the Cross, but below these, a frieze of the Humpbacked Flute Player runs round all four walls. So this joining of the traditions constantly reminds

Above: Inside St Francis' Church, Whiteriver
Below: Kateri Tekakwitha

people, "We are different - we are the same." Beside the door is another large mural of an Indian maiden. "Who can this be?" we wondered and discovered that it is Blessed Kateri Tekakwitha, the first Native American to be beatified. This is her story.

Tekakwitha - which means "She Who Puts All Things In Order" - was born in 1656, daughter of the chief of the Turtle Clan of the Mohawks of the Iroquois Nation. Kehenta, her mother, was an Algonquin captive who had been brought up among Christians and influenced by religious women who came from France to teach and minister to the French children and natives of New France. As wife of the chief, Kehenta was able to keep up the practice of her faith as well as she could in so foreign, harsh and unfriendly an atmosphere. There was someone to pray to, but no one to pray with or talk to but her little daughter. Who knows what might have happened if a smallpox epidemic had not claimed the lives of her parents and brother and left Tekakwitha an orphan at the age of four? She was adopted by her childless uncle but the smallpox had left her sickly, nearly blind and disfigured by pock marks for the rest of her short life.

As she grew up, she remembered and developed the faith her mother had begun in her and lived up to Christian ideals of loving God and caring for all His people. She had to suffer for her beliefs, fending off attacks - malicious gossip, stones, sarcasm, vicious rumours, plots to force her to marry and even a physical attack on her life. She wished only to devote her life to God, to help the sick, care for the feeble and aged and brighten the lives of those who lived in the shadow of despair and hopelessness. Her services were unobtrusive - she did not put on a show or look for recognition. She loved to be forgotten. Her self-effacing humility led to her being underestimated by so many, but who, after reflection, could see the effectiveness of her work and life.

At her baptism, she became Kateri - the "Lily of the Mohawks", adding much to the good qualities of her Mohawk and Algonquin heritage: qualities of courage, endurance, determination, and willingness to face hardship, suffering physical pain without complaint. The clear vision of her sight-dimmed eyes showed her the depth and breadth of God's love and how she, the humblest of His creatures, could make a difference to those around her; while the example of her mother's devotion to prayer blossomed in Kateri and became the foundation of all she accomplished.

It is said that when she died, the disfiguring pock marks disappeared from her face, revealing her true beauty. For a short time cures and favours were recorded and attributed to her intercession with Almighty God and to this day, Kateri's influence rekindles the awareness of personal worth and a sense of dignity among her people. She Who Puts All Things In Order, blessed and beloved of all Native Americans who know of her, continues to inspire the people of today. In a corner of St. Francis' church stands her banner, the banner of Whiteriver, which flew above their representatives at the Tekakwitha Conference, held in 1996 at Albuquerque in New Mexico. This Conference brings together Native American Catholics from every nation - Inuits from Alaska, Choctaw from Georgia, Kiowa and Sioux from the Plains, Zunis and other pueblo people and more. It is a time to meet old friends and make new ones; to share music, dancing, stories and celebrate the unity and diversity that is the Catholic faith.

Outside, in the hot Arizona sun, a flurry of activity had arisen. A coach load of people, young and old from a parish in Minnesota were mingling with young Apaches, playing games, singing songs, listening to Bible stories and trying different crafts. Some of our group joined in, enjoying the contact but when these people disappeared, we were still not clear what it was all about.

At about 5 o'clock, the Armstrongs arrived, bringing a birthday cake for Will and a very attractive sweatshirt as a present - having discovered it was his birthday yesterday, what a birthday, Will!

We began to wonder what time to expect Fr. Bernard and there were anxious glances at watches when, at last, Sr. Darlene swept into the car park in the Cibecue Sonoma estate car. Fr. Bernard had been involved in an accident on the way and although he had only suffered a bump on the nose, the minibus could not be driven and would have to be replaced the next day. After a hasty conference, our hosts arranged to take us in their transport to the supper at Cedar Creek, so we squeezed into a variety of cars and trucks and set off, out of Whiteriver towards Cibecue. Turning off the highway relatively quite soon, we passed a large wooden-framed building in the course of construction. This, we were told, is going to be the new St. Anthony's Church of Cedar Creek, replacing the old wooden church, which had fallen down; and what a pity it was that we would not be there to see it finished. We bounced along a bumpy, twisty track for what seemed like miles and miles, although it was probably not quite that far and arrived at the clearing that is the Armstrong's campsite, the place where Janell had had her Sunrise Dance.

Family members and friends were already there, greeting us shyly and welcoming us to the campfire and all around food was being unpacked or prepared for cooking. We recognised and greeted those we had last seen at Alton Castle - Teresa, Margaret, Janell and Reagan, Darren, Frank and Armadio, they really were old friends. While the feast was being set, Reagan Sr. asked us if we would like to see the waterfall, which was one of the sacred places. Kath, Rachel and the two Catherines, Paul and Will stayed behind and incidentally learned how to make frybread. The rest of us followed our guides, at a brisk pace, through the wilderness and I remember wondering where a waterfall could possibly fall, in this flat land. Yet looking around as we loped along, there were signs of water devastation everywhere, without any river or stream. The sandy ground bore evidence of swirling torrents, the bleached trunks of trees and fallen, whitened branches. The chaos of debris spoke of flood but all was dry, dry as a bone; sparse, dusty grasses crackling underfoot as we strove to keep up. This was the end of the dry season; soon the rains would begin with thunder, lightning and flash floods, this land would be under water.

Then, at last, there was the river, trickling and burbling over its stony bed, running very low at this time of the year, but with dark, deep pools under the overhanging trees. There, too, was the waterfall, not high, but beautifully flowing from rock to rock in fluid curves. When the floods were raging, it would be quite a sight. Just below the waterfall, the riverbank was grassy and the water deeper. Here, we were told, the men put up the sweat lodges for this was a sacred place, beside the running water. The light was beginning to fade and the return trip to the campsite seemed to be shorter, which was as well as dusk is but a blink at this latitude. The feast was ready. Around the clearing, tables had been set bearing all manner of food; some of which was quite surprising, spaghetti bolognaise for instance! There were salads, varieties of beans, hot dogs, slices of watermelon and other delicacies, which could not be identified, as it was now dark. To drink there was water, cherryade, Coca Cola and Apache tea; this latter was a herb tea and pleasant to drink. Around the campfire the Mothers sat, cooking frybread, burgers and sausages, while the many children, from toddlers to teenagers, threaded their ways, inconspicuously from fire to food and to drinks. We sat and stood, balancing our laden plates, and talked and talked. Familiar faces loomed up from out of the darkness into the flickering firelight, chatter and laughter floating out among the trees. We learned that the Armstrongs raised cattle on this land and this was a campsite they often used for family get-togethers. When they felt like getting away from it all, they would come out into this wilderness and spend some time living in the old ways, teaching the children by their example, the ways things used to be done.

Fr. Bernard appeared and, after much solicitous and jokey enquiries, assured us all that he really was unhurt and would go to get another minibus for us in the morning. When the food was eaten and the fire's dying embers were beginning to dim the clearing, everyone squeezed into the cars and trucks, wobbling and bumping back to the highway and home to Whiteriver.

It was still early evening for us, so, those with some energy left, decided to see what night life Whiteriver had to offer. They had strict instructions to stay together and be back no later than 10.30pm. They were back much earlier than that, however, because there is no nightlife. No clubs, no pubs, no cinemas, no coffee bars, in fact the only entertainment was basketball matches at the Memorial Hall between youth teams and an "H-Mart", where you could buy buckets of Coke.

This lack of what today's youth deem so necessary to relieve the dread boredom, became insignificant and we quickly found that life can exist without going out and spending money. Evenings became a time to relax and talk together and this is something, at which we excel - talking. We could sit for hours in serious discussion, we often "put the world to rights", we discovered that Paul and Will were a perfect double act and that Catherine knew absolutely everything there is to know about Star Trek and all its intervening generations. At last we had time to get to know each other, to find out just what we had in common and what was so vitally individualistic. There was gentle leg pulling and some brilliant humour. We appreciated what a good stroke it was to bring Rachel's guitar, although Stephen made the most use of it. In those unplanned, casual evenings we bonded into one unit, we truly liked each other in a comfortable, caring way. How easy it is to get out of dependence on television and CDs, computer games and just hanging around.

The next day, Thursday, turned out to be one of the most important days of the whole exchange. Without a minibus until midday, we were to walk to the local high school to see something of the Apache education system and to be met by Fr. Bernard in time to drive, in our new transport, to the Tribal Centre for an interview with the Tribal Chairman. As we would not have time to return to the Retreat Centre for lunch, we had to carry it with us. This also necessitated early rising to prepare an adequate picnic for twelve. Kath had voted herself in charge of food as well as shopping and soon had organised the polystyrene cool box full to the brim with sustenance and a gallon of water. Those willing boys carried everything - and it was heavy. It was also very hot, although it was only 9.30am when we set out to walk the couple of miles down the road.

Alchesay High School, its campus well defined by chain-link fencing, snuggles in the shadow of Bear Mountain. It is a low, sprawling building that has seen a few years of hundreds of pupils rattling around inside and is neither spanking new nor seriously dilapidated. Jim Best, quarter Cherokee, Counsellor and Principal

Sports Coach met us. He took us round, showing us classrooms, the old gymnasium - where dances and proms are held, and, what impressed our group, the computer room. We sat down and listened while Jim explained the school system and because so many of the Returners were still engaged in education it was particularly interesting. The pupils at Alchesay High are aged from 13 to 21 and, whereas the school was built for 400+, there are now 700+ on role. All the usual school subjects are taught in mixed ability classes of 30, an emphasis being put on Information Technology - hence the well provided computer facilities.

What is significant is that pupils speak both Apache and English but neither language with the richness of phraseology and vocabulary they both possess. They resort to slang and cliche and therefore they can find written work difficult. This is one of the main areas of concern; the others being poor school attendance; obesity and drug and substance abuse - this all sounds familiar to us. The staff is mostly Anglo-Americans who are employed by the Tribe, working for the Tribe. Jim Best said that he just considers that he works for the kids and only the kids. He keeps right out of politics, which are so complex you just don't want to know! Many of the teachers stay on during the vacation, running summer schools and sports camps.

As is the way, these days, strategies are constantly being tried to solve or at least ameliorate the particular problems of the school. Many of the academic shortcomings hinge on the inadequate literacy of the students, even the most able are at least two years adrift in reading. So a sustained Silent Reading time is being tried where everyone, teachers included, reads to themselves, something that interests them, for half an hour every day. Thus showing that reading really is for everyone, that no one is so clever that they do not need or enjoy reading.

The other strategies for tackling problem areas filled out youngsters with admiration and envy! Jim proudly showed us round the new sports hall and its attendant facilities, recently built beside the school. There were young people on the basketball court, as were entered the new building, so we were taken to see the weight training rooms, where Jim explained that one of the problems with his students is obesity. Deficient diet and a great lack of exercise cause this. The diet deficient because junk food is so instantly accessible these days and old style, sparse but nutritious, meals are no longer the norm in many households; it is so much easier to fill up with crisps, burgers, biscuits and sweets. Who would want to walk anywhere when you can pack into a car or truck; or toil over daily activities when there are labour saving machines to take the effort out of work? These are problems with which we are all too familiar; young people growing up so overweight they are unable to enjoy a reasonable life of activity. Alchesay High School has a programme of weight training and body-building to reawaken a feeling of physical well being and fitness because fitness is the passport to the basketball teams. It is at basketball that the Apache really shine. It is a game so well suited to the old traditional instincts of aggression, ruthlessness, strategy and athleticism, a game that they can win, be victorious over their opponents; it is a game that restores their pride. However, to be in the team you must be fit and to keep fit you must be out of the drug scene, not involved in substance abuse and avoid alcohol. All of these afflictions are around in force to tempt the vulnerable young. The team coaches, well trained in spotting transgressors, are ruthless in dropping anyone from the team who lapses from this strict regime, however talented and vital they might be. So the message gets absorbed and priorities established - the Team Is First and everyone strives to be a member of one of the many teams run for boys and girls of every age group. The success of this strategy is only achieved through the dedication of the whole school to making it work and although some pupils still take off and roam away, at times, in the restless, Apache fashion, sport at the high school manages to hold the majority.

We asked if all the pupils are Apache. There are five white pupils, one black and one Hispanic. How many go on to higher education? One third of last year's seniors gained entry to colleges. Where do they go? There is a community college on the reservation; some students go to colleges off the reservation in the cities; one

Top: Alchesay High School
Middle: Aidan & Fran represented Britain at 2 on 2 basketball
Bottom: Meeting the Tribal Chairman, Mr Ronnie Lupe

even went to the Veterinary College in Colorado. Sadly, many students do not function well, away from home and may drop out of higher education. They find life too difficult without their family near. If they have some family contact near to the college they do make the effort to stick it out and return to the reservation as soon as they can, with their qualifications. Does living off the reservation in the city, change the Apache at all? Yes, was the reply. They quickly find out all about racial prejudice. They are aware of people constantly watching them, suspecting them of stealing, suspicious of everything they do, or don't do. In some quarters there is open resentment of all minorities, but especially Apaches, white people ruthlessly stigmatising the whole nation, wrongly believing that they are living on state welfare. Life for reservation Apaches can be so desperately miserable, they just go home.

We went down to the courts, where the summer sports school members were taking a breather and listening to coaching points. We were introduced to the class for some of the girl's teams and were challenged to a two on two session. A hasty discussion propelled Aidan and Fran to carry the flag for Britain and, I am sorry to say, we didn't hold out much hope, but we knew they would do their best. After all, they were not really dressed for a sporting experience - Fran was wearing a long skirt and totally unsuitable shoes. Of course, if we'd known we were to be challenged, well, it would have been different! However we were in for a revelation, in spite of their obvious disadvantages, Fran and Aidan were pretty good. They held their own, they intercepted, they dribbled skilfully, working together with impressive lay-ups they gave a display our nation could be proud of and, although they were finally defeated by only one basket, honour was saved on both sides.

What a very splendid sports hall this is, all new and sparkling, with its tiers of spectator seating, its sprung floors, its changing facilities, its techno-control system. The building stands out in its terracotta and turquoise, up to date design; it blends into the local environment and is a triumph of low key architecture.

Who funds the High School? Basically, it is funded from Federal

Aid to Native Americans, although finance does have to come in from many different sources. The Tribal Council provided the finance for the sports building. The money had been raised for the high school and after consultation, it had been spent on the new sports complex. Jim said, wryly, "We desperately need more classrooms and books, but the sports complex won the battle." When the choice is between something that brings honour and prestige and prestige and something that is difficult to perceive as immediately beneficial, it is not hard to see which choice appeals.

At last it was lunchtime and we went into the school canteen to eat our picnic and drink from the many water fountains that were available all around the school. It was exceedingly hot outside. Internally satisfied and refreshed, we found ourselves a good place to be seen and picked up by Fr. Bernard in the new minibus and set off for the Tribal Centre; unaware that the meeting with the Tribal Chairman was going to be one of the most momentous encounters of the whole Exchange.

The Tribal Centre is a modern, air-conditioned building; the constant trilling of telephones and the busy receptionists at the desk testify to the complex administration of the reservation. After a short wait, during which we made many visits to the public drinking fountains, strategically placed around the reception area, we entered the Chairman's office to meet Mr. Ronnie Lupe, the elected head of the White Mountain Apaches.

He sat at his black marble-topped desk, behind him, the flag of the United States of America, the Arizona State flag and the Great Seal flag of the White Mountain Apache. After the introductions, we presented a civic greeting from the Lord Mayor of Stoke-on-Trent and a message from Lord Stafford to him, as representative of the Apache people. In his reply Mr. Lupe welcomed us and said the Apache appreciate visitors from anywhere in the world and that we were a unique, a special group; because of our youth, we represented tomorrow's people. It is important to recognise that all people have a spiritual side to their nature that everyone can recognise - it is one of willingness to try to understand each other, to have a good attitude and respect for all people. No words are needed when the feeling comes from our hearts.

When the Europeans settled in America they had the desire to get rid of all the Indians from the land. They tried many ways and eventually decided to take the Indians from their own lands and relocate them elsewhere, to break them away from their roots, suppress their customs, language and way of life so that they would disappear forever. The methods they used were mean and cruel and in some ways paralleled the Holocaust.

"But they never did that to the White Mountain Apache," said Ronnie Lupe. "We always ran off. They never got us off our land. They tried. We are still here." Many battles have been lost and some have been won, but the White Mountain Apache still have their own land and their own government. They have their own judicial and criminal codes, make their own laws, raise their own taxes, manage their own economy and organise their own social codes. This makes the US government uneasy - an independent nation within their midst! The war still goes on. "We cannot wear the same shoes as Geronimo, Cochise, Mangus Colorados, we cannot replace them and that kind of leadership, these days. But we can hold the balance for stability, while blocking interference from outside that threatens our traditional values, our language, dance and ceremonies. All these things were outlawed by the US government at one time."

Many of the ceremonies are private to the Apache communities but one that is acknowledged widely and is known to peoples far away from Apacheland is the Sunrise Dance. In this ceremony the Creator, God - or "Usen" in the Apache language, says to an innocent young girl, "You're it. I'm sending the most powerful Man to earth through you."

"Why me?" she asks. "There are stronger people here, better qualified people. Why me?"

"Do not fear," says Creator. "You're it. You are the important one who holds the future generations in your hands."

He has taken an unknown, an innocent, the least of all the people to work his ways. You would think he would take the strongest, the most powerful, but no. It is from the young, the innocent that the greatest power comes. She has the power to bring all peoples together. She has nothing to offer only her humility and simplicity. That is real power, it gathers everyone together and blesses everyone each in their own way and in their own need.

"We have done this from time immemorial," said the Tribal Chairman. "When we did not know that there was anything beyond the great oceans, we had never heard that a similar question was asked two thousand years ago of a young innocent girl. This is very remarkable to us.

When we come together for our ceremonies we are remembering to say thank you, thank you for our beautiful land, our way of life. We invite people to come to our land with a lot of respect, a lot of experiences of their own way of life, their own history and their love of their own land. For we are in love with our land, our roots. We will never be torn apart, away from it. We would much rather die. We would much rather die and say, 'It's a beautiful day to die, anyway.' This is an echo that comes down to us from those old days; we are a humble people, but disturb us and we rebel a bit! We no longer use the lance, the bow and arrow. We use paper!" Ronnie Lupe pointed to a stack of documents on his desk.

The major talking point of the moment is the water dispute. The massive and rapid expansion and development of the cities of Arizona and their surrounding areas is putting a devastating ecological strain on the land. Urban pollution is one big problem but far more serious than even that is the critical abstraction of water. The demands of huge conurbations like Phoenix and even far away California have so belittled the great Colorado River, that it is only a trickle into the Gulf of California. Now expanding Tucson, its own surface water exhausted, takes its water from the White Mountains. The White Mountains, with their rainfall and snowfall, are the only recharge for the whole water system. There has been an abundance of water stored in the vast, subterranean Coconino Aquifer for millions of years. This aquifer and its companion volcanic aquifer underlie the northern half of the reservation and stretch east into New Mexico, north, almost to Utah and west to Flagstaff. The 26 lakes and 400 miles of rivers of the reservation that replenish land, baked in the soaring summer temperatures, are able to maintain a constant flow, due to this stored groundwater. Off the reservation, to the north, certain tributaries of the Little Colorado River and Silver Creek have dried up since the US government, with legal language, permits the continual pumping of water from the 100 wells on the reservation and 500 wells outside the reservation. A natural system that has balanced the land for millions of years is being systematically pumped dry to water the golf courses and fill the private swimming pools of the city dwellers and increase the profits of Water Companies. Litigation is the only weapon, not only of the Apache, but also of all concerned people and legal battles, whether in the State Courts or eventually in the Supreme Court of the USA, take money - and they take more time than there is. For when the fast diminishing store of water is gone, it can never be replaced. Then the precious land will die. Not only the Apache will die - everything will die. The war goes on!

    The Chairman explained the symbolism of the Great Seal of the White Mountain Apache Tribe. In the Apache Creation Myth, Usen blew his breath into the darkness to begin His creation, so the background to the seal is black. The four cardinal points are represented as four stars, white for the north, black for the east, blue for the south and yellow for the west. The zigzag mystically contains the sacred numbers and the 32 ways to cure people in healing ceremonies and this zigzag can also be seen in the headdresses of the Crown Dancers. The sacred, snowcapped mountain, Mount Baldy and the river running through are the land and life itself, the uniquely Apache water pot holds the "life-sustainer". The elk represents the animals; the traditional home, the wickiup, represents the people and the tree stands for all other living species that have an equal right to exist upon the land. The lightning connects the Creator with the land and the eagle feathers represent the Indian prayers to God - the same in all Indian nations. The blue sky is the Apache roof above their heads. And the rainbow? The rainbow represents peace and tranquillity of mind for everyone and their hope for the future. This, the Apache have known for ever but they are awed to find that other peoples, all over the world, hold a similar idea about the rainbow.

This meeting we had with the Tribal Chairman is considered one of the most significant happenings of the whole Exchange. We were so impressed by this rotund, silver-haired, grandfather figure, in his jeans and stripy shirt, who could laugh and joke with us and yet still retain his position of wise, respected elder with dignity. He explained the Great Seal, perfect in every detail and colour, made from 16 local stones, inlaid into the marble of his desk.

"They said it couldn't be done, it was impossible," he said. "But I showed that, after many prayers and trying many ways, it could be done. I have done it! It is not just for show, not just to be clever. I have done it to show that with a positive mind, you can do impossible things." This is the way forward for the Apache people.

The Tribal Chairman had given us much to ponder as we made our way to the Tribal Council's Rainbow Centre. This substantial building is home to the drug and alcohol rehabilitation programme. The well-known Native American alcoholism is a genetic problem. There is a missing factor in their genetic make-up that renders them unable to cope with the smallest amount of alcohol. So when life's burdens result in a turn to drink, it does not take much to be in the grip of the addiction. But here in comfort and security, those casualties of today's society are helped back to the way of life without dependence. The dedicated workers counsel and encourage, propose strategies for coping, lend a shoulder to cry on to people who have touched the very bottom and have nowhere else to turn but to grasp the hand held out to them. Even in this seemingly sensitive land, a lack of purpose in life, feelings of low self-worth, family problems, unemployment, poverty and unreliable handouts that insult the dignity, fuel the drift into the oblivion of alcoholism and substance abuse. At the Rainbow Centre, there is a chance to get medical help, advice from those who have been there themselves, support to keep on task and the facilities to rebuild the fragile structure of lives gone astray. Success is there and so too is failure - some people are straightened out while some lapse and lapse again. It always takes a special kind of unsung hero to

do this kind of work. Returning home, we had so much to occupy our minds, that we very gratefully welcomed the tasty tacos quickly prepared by Teresa and Janell, who had been our constant and valued companions all day.

We had pretty well got a detailed picture of how Apacheland functions today, but how does it tie in with our old notions of Red Indians? The chance was to come on Friday when Fr. Bernard picked us up at 9.45am, and took us to the nearby Fort Apache.

There is so much unknown about the early history of the Native American peoples. This we do know: they came from Asia at the end of the last Ice Age, having been pushed ever north and east, across the land mass, by the pressure of migrating peoples contesting the land. The fleeing people crossed the land bridge from today's Russia into today's Alaska until the rising waters from the melting ice, covered what is now the Bering Strait. For thousands of years those now safely on the shores of the empty continent were isolated. A continent, empty only of humans, for the immigrants found as they moved south and east, that it was a continent of abundant resources for those skilful enough to appreciate them.

They identified themselves as "the people" - a species inhabiting the land along with other species; the trees, the deer, the fish etc. They lived on the land; they did not own the land. The tribes and families spread, gradually, over thousands of years to fill not only North America but South America too, each tribe or nation adapting to a particular area and developing its own customs, language and identity. As in the other populous continents, America became a patchwork of nationalities, each keen to maintain their independence; protect their own boundaries, and even extend them. They strove to enhance their own life style; seeing the need to communicate with and to trade with their neighbours in spite of language difficulties and mutual suspicion. But in all this time, until the last 500 years, they lived without contact with the rest of the world; they believed themselves to be the only people in the world.

It is interesting to study the culture and find it so rich; the social structures and find them so complex; the philosophy and find it so spiritual, when we, in our ignorance, thought there was nothing there. It demonstrates the power of oral tradition that, although Native Americans had no written language, the thousands of years of their history still lives and, related in story and allegory, through the overlapping generations, is less susceptible to error than the intermittent interpretation of the written word.

We know that the Apache are a branch of the Athabascan tribes of northwestern Canada, who migrated south about a thousand years ago. They were scattered from West Texas, across southern New Mexico into south eastern Arizona; north into southern Kansas and southern Colorado; and south into the Mexican states of Chihuahua and Sonora. Soon after their arrival, they split into a number of subtribes or bands, each developing their own distinctive dialect. Although they were all Apaches, there was often fierce rivalry between the different groups that could become very bitter. The most fearsome were the Chiricahuas of the Arizona/New Mexico borders and other notable bands were the White Mountain Apaches and the Cibecue group, the San Carlos, the Warm Springs and the Coyoteros.

Each Apache group was composed of extended families, or clans - basically social, economic and political units. The leadership of the clan was usually matrilineal - passing through the female line. The head woman determined the clan's territory and organised the social and economic status; the headman was chosen informally for his leadership abilities and fighting skills. Sometimes the headman was the leading woman's husband, but not necessarily so, what counted most was his ability. The most charismatic leader could unite clans and command great respect within the tribe, however he was not seen as the "chief" in the conventional way we think of. When a son married, he went to live in his mother-in-law's camp and his obligations were to his wife's family; marriage within one's own clan is still forbidden.

The Apache lived by hunting, gathering and by trading and raiding. They never did take to a settled way of life like their nearby Athabascan cousins, the Navajo. Perhaps because they felt threatened by their dispossessed neighbours, they gained a reputation for ferocity and became renowned remorseless warriors and guerrilla fighters. Indeed their very name Apache translates as "enemy" to their foes. They warred, endlessly against the settled, agricultural Pueblos, the Pimas and Papagos and against the Comanches and lived a restless, nomadic life in their mountain and desert homeland.

We have been often asked about the wigwams or the tepees and whether we would be living in one. Apaches do not make these. Their traditional shelter is the wickiup, built from a framework of light but strong branches, covered with brushwood. Once established in a campsite, they could be left when the tribe moved on and quickly repaired the next time a group passed that way. The range of the Apache was from the flat desert to the deeply wooded mountains and they moved to suit the seasons - the heat of summer and the snows of winter.

This nomadic life of subsistence hunting and gathering, trading, raiding and warring went on, unrecorded until the arrival of the Spanish towards the end of the 17th century, when with cross and sword, the invaders set about converting and civilising the native populations.

Spanish attention was first drawn to the more peaceable, Pueblo Indians in their settlements and a modicum of success was achieved; mission fields were tilled, mission stock was tended and the mission church attracted its congregation. This agricultural life was definitely not a life for the Apache and a merry game was enacted as they defied all the attempts of the Spanish and later the Mexicans to conquer them.

In desperation the Mexican authorities resorted to the old Spanish custom of paying bounties for the scalps of undesirable Apaches, but this in turn led to an upsurge of "backyard barbers" - scurrilous opportunists from all walks of life cashed in on this bonanza. Who could tell whether the scalp was from a hostile or a friendly warrior, or for that matter, from a woman or child? Who could tell and who cared whether the scalp was Indian or Mexican? The bounty paid was just the same. Whole villages of Mexicans were exterminated for their scalps and the money that could be made from them, the Arizona/Mexico border was inflamed with hatred and the subjugation of the Apache no nearer a conclusion.

When American pioneers arrived in Arizona in the mid 1850s, at the end of the US/Mexican War, the first two settlements were the mining towns of Tucson and Tubac, in the heart of the Apache lands and the Apaches welcomed the newcomers as allies against the Mexicans. This state of affairs did not last long, though. Scorning international boundaries, the Apache were accustomed to crossing into the Chihuahua and Sonora states of Mexico as they had always done - for trading and raiding. When Anglo lumbermen ambushed a homeward-bound raiding party and the Apaches had wreaked their terrible revenge, a three-cornered fight had developed and Cochise, leader of the Chiricahua Apaches, rose to power.

A big issue in the settlement of the new south western territories was the government policy of controlling all the native populations in reservations. The maintenance of this control was by re-garrisoning the old Spanish forts and establishing new ones. The New Arizonans felt safer with the Army at hand to protect them as they developed their mining, lumber and stock-rearing businesses and all the infrastructure of a new state, but the Apache grew more and more dissatisfied with a life of confinement. Of course, the land reserved for them was the least desirable, desert terrain centred on San Carlos and could not possible sustain the numbers put there. The extra food that had to be delivered was poor and inadequate; it suffered in regularity and quality and was fraught with distribution scams. Frustrated warriors resorted to the old ways of the nomadic hunter and raider to sustain their families. The San Carlos reservation was obviously too small and finally the Government agreed to extend its boundaries to include the White Mountains. With glee, Apaches relate that the authorities mistakenly thought that the extra territory they were giving was desert, like San Carlos, whereas the White Mountains are among the most beautiful and productive parts of Arizona. This was, perhaps, the only stroke of good fortune they ever had in all their dealings with the US government. Too often, prejudice, ignorance and greed-driven trickery was meted out by the White Man, answered in turn with ruthless vengeance from the Red Man. Cochise continued to resist the forced confinement on a reservation with his renegade bands until he finally accepted a peace treaty, which was honoured by the Chiricahuas until his death.

However, the peace was an uneasy one; for the Apache still resented reservation life. Living in, for them, such close proximity to their disliked cousins; unable to find enough food for their families and denied the right to roam and hunt as had been their custom; dependence on their captors was an unbearable humiliation. The status of warrior was slighted by putting farming implements into his hand and expecting him to cultivate the patch of land around his home, something that had never been in his culture. It suited the "Tucson Ring" of merchants to capitalise on this unrest - even actively to promote it, for where there were Indian troubles, more troops would come and that meant a boom in business. More soldiers would need more horses and more food for both. The Tucson Ring could provide whatever was needed. This situation was not unknown to some of the more conscientious officers and it must be said that not all were insensitive to the injustices being perpetrated; they strove to be evenhanded in their dealings.

It was in the summer of 1858 that Mexican irregular troops massacred a camp of defenceless Bedonkohe Apache women and children, stealing supplies and arms. This drove the remaining warriors to join up with the Chiricahuas and in this vengeful band was Geronimo, who had lost his mother, his wife and his three children in the attack. For the next 28 years, Geronimo grew in skill and reputation as a charismatic leader and many disaffected young warriors joined him on the warpath, off the reservation. His band of renegades ranged all over the territory with their raiding, covering great distances at speed over the rough terrain, creeping up silently upon their enemies and fading away into the security of their mountain hideouts.

During this time, government forces had pursued a relentless campaign against them, with such scant success that they turned

Geronimo

© *Courtesy of the Arizona Historical Society/Tuscon No. 6a*

Apache Scouts with their prisoners
© *Courtesy of the Arizona Historical Society/Tuscon No.74*

to the Apaches themselves for help. The best trackers of Apaches were other Apaches and it was not difficult to recruit White Mountain Apaches into the Apache Scouts since great hatred existed between the various bands; here was an opportunity to settle some old scores while placating the authorities enough to be left alone. With the aid of the Apache Scouts, the renegades were eventually tracked down. Geronimo finally surrendered to General Miles in August 1886 on the understanding that he and his band would be transported with the rest of the tribe, for a time, to Florida and then returned to their homeland. This seemed a better prospect than a civil trial in Arizona where there was little hope from the justice handed out by the pioneers.

At no time, however, did Geronimo consider that he had surrendered unconditionally, but that was not how the government saw it. They treated Geronimo and his followers as prisoners of war and not only them. Peaceful Chiricahua and Warm Springs Apaches and even their own Apache Scouts were betrayed by government officials in far away Washington, into exile, bundled onto trains at Holbrook and transported hundreds of miles to alien Florida. The proud, fierce, mountain peoples suffered in the hot, humid, lowlands! Such was their obvious distress, that they were moved from Fort Marion, Florida to Fort Sills in Oklahoma - always as prisoners - always confined in Army Forts. Far greater suffering was endured by the Apache Scouts - not only were they unjustly imprisoned, but they were uncaringly confined with the very people for whose downfall they were responsible.

Even when Geronimo died, in 1909, he and the Apaches were still captives, warily guarded by the Army, treated with suspicion, loathing and contempt by the rest of the populace. When they were finally allowed to return to Arizona, in 1913, it was grudgingly, without government support - they must make their way as best they could, or give in and be swallowed up by modern America. Today, Geronimo's name is known to warriors the world over, synonymous with courage and tenacity. It is the battle cry of armies and his name echoes as paratroopers jump from their transport plane. Who remembers the names of any of the government officials

Fort Apache

who decided Apache fate? Who remembers the names of any of the military that chased them for so long?

So here we Returners were, at Fort Apache, just a few miles out of Whiteriver, off to the left when you are heading west towards Cedar Creek. The fort had been built on flat, high land with a good view of the surrounding country. At first, in 1869, it was just a camp for the 1st US Cavalry and, as it developed into a permanent military post, became Fort Apache in 1879. Military duties were mostly guarding the telegraph lines and new roads that traversed the country and supporting the Indian Agent responsible for maintaining some sort of order among the tribes. The only real clash came when the troopers were called upon to quell the followers of Nakaidoklini at the Battle of Cibecue Creek, in 1881 and to repel the subsequent attack on the Fort by a large band of Apaches. The last actual battle fought between the Army and the Apache was in 1882 at Chevalon Creek, called the Battle of Big Dry Wash. Most of the troops had left Fort Apache by 1922. It was abandoned as a military installation in 1924 and handed over to the Department of the Interior for use as Theodore Roosevelt Indian School. The large adobe brick building, with boarded up windows we deduced to be the barracks of the troopers, while a little way off were the separate buildings of the officer's quarters, the adjutant's office, the guard house and cavalry barns. The large empty space must have been the parade ground and a little way off is the cemetery - the final resting place for both solders and Indian Scouts.

Now Fort Apache is on the National Register of Historic Places and even more significantly, is on the list of The World Monuments Watch as one of the world's 100 irreplaceable, endangered cultural heritage sites. Slowly, Fort Apache is being restored as an Apache Culture Centre and Museum for, unlike many similar forts, it is not a reconstruction. Its original buildings still stand although they are in need of sympathetic repair. The curator of the museum was away, unfortunately, but entering one officer's house we discovered Clarissa and Desiree, threading minute beads for Apache jewellery. They were our museum guides and showed us around Nowika'

Bagowa - "House of Our Footprints" - where the exhibits are displayed in cases in the several rooms. There were Apache artefacts from distant times - flint arrowheads, pottery and tools. There was war regalia - lances and shields, and Sunrise Dance paraphernalia, including the buckskin serape and soft buckskin boots. There were all kinds of household and agricultural implements and a collection of burden baskets, which gave us a better idea of a true size as the ones we had were scaled down souvenirs. We saw a quern that had been used in the olden days for grinding corn for flour.

One section of the exhibition showed objects used by the military during their stay in this place - rifles and sabres and also little homely things, like a small sewing kit, things used by soldiers, far from home. On the walls were many, many photographs of soldiers and Apaches. Old faded monochrome pictures they were, in the stiff poses of early photographs; grim-faced Apache Scouts and serious, pompous officials, all posing in large groups. There were also photographs of Apache women in their camp dresses that were the same then, as they are today.

Quite a section was devoted to the Apache Scouts and we quizzed Clarissa about them. How did the Apaches feel about these Apache men working for the military? Did the Apaches want Geronimo to escape? Why did they help to track him down? Geronimo and his renegades were not White Mountain Apache, they were Chiricahuas and Warm Springs Apache and there was enmity between these tribes. If the White Mountain Apache scouted for the soldiers, their families would be left alone and as they would be paid, there would be food for their families. Living on the reservation was very hard for the people because they could not go where they wanted to go, to hunt and to trade. There was never enough food and Apache families were always in danger of ill treatment. It was better to be on the same side as the military - particularly as they were living so near, on Apache land. "We can't do anything about those days," said Clarissa.

Our guides then took us to see the Apache village that was on land below the fort. We followed them down roughly cut steps to the bottom of a ravine and over a worn, but trustable wooden bridge, spanning the swiftly running stream which is the north fork of the White River. Up the raised bank of the stream and along a narrow path for a short way, the Apache village has been reconstructed and is still used at times these days. There are three wickiups standing quite near each other and a large sun shelter with log seats for the villagers to use when the sun is at its fiercest. A little way away from the dwellings are the small firepits where the cooking is done.

It was not at all difficult to sit in the shade and think yourself back into the living village of a few generations ago. The wickiups with their fresh coverings of brushwood, still green and thick, are alive with children running, playing, calling, laughing and crying, while grandmothers sit patiently inside or under the sun shelter, gossiping quietly, fingers every busy with work to be done. Older children and mothers collect vegetables and herbs from the surrounding countryside, filling their burden baskets with whatever is in season. The burden baskets, trimmed with tin jungles, sound out musically, enabling the gatherers to keep in touch with each other and at the same time warning wild animals of the presence of humans so that neither would startle the other. Men and boys hunt together for rabbit, turkey and other small game, the skill being passed from generation to generation. Perhaps the biggest fire pit is only used for big communal meals - not for everyday and all around there is plenty of deadfall wood for the camp fires set a little way away from the dwellings. So here is everything necessary for sustaining life - the nearby stream for drinking water, the shelters to sleep in, shade for the heat of the day, food available close at hand and security of a family social system which has a place for everyone. When food is plentiful there is time for other pursuits like planning family events, producing clothes and useful objects, making jewellery from coloured beads and porcupine quills, working hides into supple fine leather, fashioning weapons for hunting, for raiding parties or for war. But life is always precarious; food is not always readily at hand, some seasons are harsh and disaster can strike at any time. Birth, death, sickness and accidents,

Above: Fort Apache Village - 2 wickiups and the sun shelter
Below: Fort Apache Village - Clarissa beside the sweat lodge

arguments, disagreements and family splits are all here, too. There is an element of harshness and cruelty woven into the life also, an inflicting of suffering and an indifference of feeling for the victim. A society so close to Nature, takes on Nature's wildest aspects too and, over the centuries, I guess, Man has embellished these for his own ends.

What community in any place, in any time is not familiar with these trials and tribulations of human existence? What else can people do, but hang on and survive? Hang on and survive and make something distinctive of whatever they are, of who they are.

Clarissa showed us some of the edible and medicinal plants that still grow and are still used around the village and we wondered if the village would have had a medicine man. The knowledge of common medicine would have been widespread - like our knowing about dock leaves for nettle stings - but for more serious conditions a medicine man would be sought. He would not only cater for medical needs with healing ceremonies, but also for the other ills that plague human beings, involving complex counselling and consultation with the Creator. Over the thousands of years, a philosophy has evolved which seeks to make sense of why we are here and where we are going and how. It is a theme to be found in all culture, the world over. The medicine man, or woman, is a shaman, a priest and it is he or she who leads the prayers, heals the sickness or controls the ceremonies. The role is one of great importance and the influence, for good or evil, depends on their talent and the quality of their learning. The Apache, no less than other people, or perhaps more than other people, have a spiritual dimension which is profound and heart wrenching when you take the trouble to investigate a little further than the obvious.

A little apart from the village we inspected the frame of a sweat lodge, while Clarissa explained what sweat lodges are all about. The sweat lodge is only for men and is used for self-purification before important ceremonies and momentous occasions. The frame is covered with brushwood and hides or tarpaulins so that it is tightly sealed. Rocks are heated in a fire and carried into the lodge. When the men involved are seated, water is poured over the hot rocks, creating a scalding steam that fills the small sealed room. As the sweat pours out of them, the men chant prayers to the beat of the drum and when it becomes almost unbearable, the entrance flap is raised and they crawl out to refresh themselves in the river. All the badness that has been sweated out is now washed away in the cool running water - which is why sweat lodges are beside streams and rivers and why streams, rivers and even springs are sacred places. Besides providing the essential and life-sustaining water for creation, they absorb the sins of the penitents without being tainted themselves. Several sessions in the sweat lodge and the river are endured, each more difficult and taxing than the last, the drumming, and the chanting having a mesmerising effect. During this time the men pray and offer their suffering for those who need their prayers. The whole experience is physically extremely hard, but the effect of spiritual offering and cleansing speaks of power beyond the mundane. "Yes," said Clarissa. "This sweat lodge and others are still used." And we understood, at last, the significance of the sweat lodge beside the sacred waterfall at Cedar Creek.

During the steep climb out of the ravine up the zigzag flight of steps we noticed rusty iron bedsteads and many rusty tin cans lying among the trees. These, we were told, had been thrown down there when the US soldiers finally left Fort Apache. It is not clear who threw them there - the departing soldiers or the jubilant Apaches.

There is a melancholy air about the old fort, even as it struggles to become a cultural centre and museum; as if the sadness and badness, of times not so long ago, still linger and a sigh of regret whispers around the forlorn buildings. When we asked how today's Apache felt about those times of strife at the end of the last century and most of this one, the answer was without rancour. "Those things happened, we were not there, nothing we can do will change what happened, so we must look forward and make things better in the future." So they are not dwelling on the past, is it we who are still haunted by guilt at the injustice done?

It was now near midday and Fr. Bernard drove us north, out of the reservation to Show Low, a small town where we could buy mementoes and gifts and experience something of everyday American Arizona. On this journey and the others we took up this road, there were cries of "There's a bear...and another bear," from the back of the minibus. But although we reacted quickly, those at the front never saw one. Which makes you think, doesn't it? After tucking in to fries and burgers at the "Jack in the Box" we spent a happy couple of hours wandering around the shops. Here was another "Basha's" supermarket, a Walmart, a JC Penney's and several small gift shops. We bought our postcards and stamps and the cowboy hats that were high on our lists of priorities. We noted those items that could be a gift possibility when we came back for serious shopping and that there was a sale on where the coolest of trainers were offered at a bargain price - less that half what you would pay at home. The economy of Show Low was about to take off in a big way.

Back at the Retreat Centre we had only a short time to get really smartened up before we were to travel up the highway again to Hon Dah, a place which translates from Apache as "Welcome", as guests of the Tribal Chairman at the Indian Pine Restaurant. There was a subtle difference to this trip, however, as Fr. Bernard was leaving the minibus in our hands; he really could not spend all his time driving us around. The thought of driving a large, unfamiliar vehicle, full of precious people on strange, right hand drive roads came as a bit of a bombshell to Fr. David. It was rather stunning and daunting to the unprepared - so it was a good thing he did not have long to worry about it! Fr. Bernard showed him the automatic controls and sat beside him as he drove us to Hon Dah, Sr. Darlene followed behind with the Cibecue Sonoma. After this baptism of fire, Fr. David did all the driving, about 1500 miles in all, and is now a thoroughly competent minibus driver. He came home with an extra accomplishment! As the other driver named on the insurance, I did get a chance to handle the minibus in the carpark - just in case a disaster struck and I was needed to drive. It never did and our travelling was smooth and almost uneventful.

Top: Beautiful Apacheland
Bottom Left: The shops at Show Low. Right: Big business at Hon Dah

Apache Exchange

The Indian Pine Restaurant is part of an extensive, commercial enterprise run by the Apache Tribal Council. In the higher mountains, at Sunrise Lake, there is a tourist sports and leisure complex and throughout the reservation there are mining, stock rearing and lumber businesses. All these provide the much needed employment and revenue. Employment is also provided in the public service sectors of education, health, law and order and the ever necessary fire fighting. Then, of course, there are the retail outlets - the supermarkets, the craft shops, the motor services, all under the control of the Tribal Council. In Hon Dah, together with the restaurant, there is the casino, so strictly controlled regarding the age limit of only over 21s, that eyes downcast, we hurried through to get into the restaurant, surreptitiously glancing at the one armed bandits with their hopeful devotees. I did not see if there were other casino games but I expect there are, for the casino is very profitable and popular with Apache adults.

The restaurant is very sophisticated and elegant, the surroundings are so pleasant and the quality of the cuisine is excellent. Although the Chairman was, unfortunately, unable to be present, each member of the group received a baseball cap with the Hon Dah logo and beautiful, enamelled Great Seal pin badges from him, to mark our visit. The wonderful meal from the help-yourself-buffet took a long time to eat and savour and even the boys came to a full stop in helping themselves. Our meal was accompanied by a coke, water, tea or coffee, as there is no alcohol on sale on the reservation. We did not miss alcohol and never had drink-driving worries in any of our travelling. So, after this memorable meal, we set off on our first solo journey into the black velvet Arizona night. It was not very late when we arrived back in Whiteriver; some stalwarts set off to the Memorial Hall for yet another basketball match and, yes, even managed another bucket of coke!

Up early the next day, Saturday, we left Whiteriver to the tunes of Matt Redman's *"The Friendship and the Fear"*, for a visit to Fr. Bernard's parish, Cibecue, and what proved to be the second of the three most wonderful experiences of the whole Exchange. One thing about travelling in Arizona is that there are not many roads to get lost on and, following the instructions given us by Fr. Bernard, Fr. David brought the minibus to a smart halt, at the designated time, on the car park of St. Catherine's Church.

Fr. Bernard and Sr. Darlene was there to meet us but the first greetings were from the dogs, Tiger and her son, Smokey. Tiger had been rescued from a life of misery and they both proved to be effective guards and faithful, affectionate companions. Apaches do not now often keep dogs as house pets. We toured the church complex around the cinder car park; there is an old adobe parish hall, the parish office, Fr. Bernard's static trailer and Sr. Darlene's similar one and the little church itself. The church is a neat red sandstone building, already becoming too small for its congregation; inside the walls are newly painted - white so that after consultation with the elders, Apache artists can paint appropriate murals. Until the themes have been decided, St. Catherine's church is a plain haven of peace and tranquillity, but with some very thought-provoking pictures on the walls. The one that takes the eye immediately is a framed print of a Native American representation of the Holy Trinity. It shows God the Father as a wise and respected elder, God the Son as a young warrior and God the Holy Spirit as a falcon. We thought an Apache had painted it, but no, we found out later that the artist is Fr. John Giuliani. This painting is very moving, exquisite in its technique, so calm and penetrating in its assertion that God is saying; "I am here for you, my people. I have always been here like this." Other pictures portray Jesus as a young Apache Brave breaking bread at the Last Supper and a lovely Apache Mary with the child Jesus. However, we were constantly drawn back to the Holy Trinity, it brings a lump to your throat just to look at it.

There had been churches in the area, on and off, since Spanish missionary times. Christianity had its appeal in quieter periods and flourished, only to be dashed down by the strife caused by ignorant prejudice and frankly dishonest double-dealing. Throughout the troubled centuries, the thread of Faith still ran; church communities were built, knocked down and rebuilt. St.

Top: St Catherine's Church, Cibecue
Middle: Sr Darlene and Fr Bernard bless the work horses
Bottom: The outskirts of Cibecue

Catherine's is one of these. There had been no resident priest for a long time and the people of Cibecue had been praying and constantly petitioning the Bishop in Gallop, to send them a priest of their own. Fr. Bernard, sent from England by his Salvatorian order to work wherever he was needed, was thinking of taking on a new challenge after 21 years of counselling and teaching in Wisconsin. The Bishop of Gallop asked him and Sr. Darlene Pienschke to consider answering the prayers of the Apache and serve their parish of Cibecue. In 1993, they made a visit to see what they might be letting themselves in for in this remote area with its inherent problems and 60% unemployment. "It was just about the worst place on earth that you would want to be," says Fr. Bernard. "So we took it."

At first they had nowhere to live, no telephone, no water supply, hardly any congregation and active hostility from the other "Christian" churches in the area. The church, itself had been cared for, but there was still a great deal of maintenance needed and so much pastoral work to be done. Help comes from the Catholic parishes of America who are able, with their donations, to subsidise the missions and, with their interest, give much needed moral support; however the necessity is great and the resource limited. From the core of Catholics who steadfastly held on to their faith, the church community of Cibecue grows steadily and with the help of many willing hands repairs have been made to the buildings and to the fabric of life itself. The parish hall is home to so many activities and St. Catherine's is now in touch with not only the rest of America but with us in Staffordshire, thousands of miles away in another world.

Certain questions really troubled us before the double Exchange even began. Should we be interfering in the Apache way of life? Were we imposing our religion on them? In the light of history, how dare we?

The answer was simple, "We understand the Message of Jesus Christ," the Apache said. "And the Message is far greater than the messengers."

Cibecue is glad to have Fr. Bernard and Sr. Darlene because, in their care, they respect the Apache culture and make an effort to incorporate tribal traditions into the Mass and into the teachings. Although the Mass is just the same as you would find anywhere in Christendom, there are subtle inclusions like the use of the drum, the blessing with sacred pollen, the turning to the four directions, the purification with sacred smoke and the use of Apache prayers and songs in the liturgy.

The response of the Apache people to the Exchange - enabling the group to make the visit to England and welcoming us to Apacheland - is evidence of an acceptance of these missionaries, but significantly more so, is their being invited to participate in ceremonies few Anglos ever see. Fr. Bernard has endured the sweat lodge with the other men preparing themselves spiritually for a Sunrise Dance and, having been asked to lead the dance, danced through eight long songs in the evening and from six o'clock the next morning until eleven-thirty. Sr. Darlene was asked to bless the Crown Dancer's crowns and both are involved in praying with the sick and dying, officiating at funerals, teaching little children, instructing the older ones; serving their parish in a considerate and sensitive way, they are warmly accepted and respected. We could sense a gentle purposefulness - a big task that is making headway and going places.

Some time that morning (who knows, or cares what time it actually was - Apaches are flexible with the time and we were becoming flexible too) Lee Ann arrived in her pick-up and so did Wayne in his, all ready to take us on a guided tour. We drove round Cibecue, noting the little houses with their surrounding patches of land, the school, the signs of commercial activity and visiting the shop, then, with the Returners in the back of the two pick-ups, we set off up into the mountains. I must confess, here, to a certain tremor of anxiety as those wild children of ours sat on the edges of the backs of the trucks in an alarmingly unsafe fashion. I thought of all the seat belts, hard hats and safety measures we are used to - you wouldn't be allowed to ride in a car park like this at home! I had a firm word with them and they just grinned and said they would be OK and they wouldn't be silly, but my heart was in my mouth for many a mile - until I joined them! The cavalcade of two pick-ups and the St. Catherine's estate threaded its way along the bumpy track, climbing steadily through the trees. Sr. Darlene and Fr. Bernard noted with concern that the leaves were already beginning to turn into their autumn colours, although it was only July; we aren't the only ones obsessed with unusual seasons, these days.

Then we stopped at a place that seemed no different from anywhere else and everyone disembarked. We followed Wayne and Lee Ann off the track, among the trees, for about 15 minutes walk until we came to a lively spring rushing down the hillside. This is White Springs, a very special, sacred place, inhabited by many spirits. I think we were too many, too noisy and too unfocussed to really benefit from the spirituality of this place until...as we were leaving, Wayne pointed to a large rock on which lay three small fish-hooks. "Someone has caught some fish, somewhere," he said. "They made a thank offering to the spirit of the spring." And for a moment we were all tuned in to that sacred place, felt its spiritual power and understood - without the need of words.

Back then to the pick-ups and away along the narrow tyre-marked tracks through the forest. Coloured ribbons had been tied to certain trees along the track, which, we were told, marked the way for the lumbermen. Slowly we drove, swaying precariously and bumping up what seemed like impossibly steep bits and sharply down rock strewn twisty bits, but climbing steadily all the while. The forest closed in on us, so still and silent. Although the trees had been mostly oaks and junipers, with low growing bushes beneath them, when we set out, the higher we went, the more Ponderosa and Pinion Pine and lack of undergrowth was evident.

Eventually the pick-ups halted and we disembarked at a suitable place for a picnic. Not many Apache are familiar with this place - it is the special, sacred Pumpkin Lake. The lake is perfectly circular and has no apparent source; no streams or springs run into it or out from it and its level never varies from season to season or from year to year. This is curious for a start. We gazed across the still,

The sacred White Springs

Top: Travelling up into the wilderness
Middle: The sacred Pumpkin Lake
Bottom: Upwards, every upwards through the forest

calm water that was entirely surrounded by pumpkin plants and reeds. Dragonflies flashed their gaudy colours among the vegetation and skimmed the surface and other insects and birds murmured their conversations while Wayne related the story that is told about this place. Many years ago, at the time the Apache now estimate to be when Jesus was living on earth, the personification of the one they now call Jesus, in the Apache tongue, came to this place and washed himself in its waters. Since then, the waters are believed to be holy and have strong healing powers and this is the place to come for those who are in desperate need of spiritual and physical healing. Also Wayne said, there is a place near this lake where the footprint of Jesus is embedded in the rock, it is a real print of a man's foot. The sounds of voices could be heard through the trees and soon a family party joined us; they had heard that we would be there. So we had company for our picnic.

Most of the food eaten and half the water drunk, our journey continued upwards, stopping for a view of the Blue Lake which is just a beautiful mountain pool in its own right - but not a special, holy place. The forested mountains have a curious atmosphere of life and completeness; everything getting on with its own life - growing, feeding and just being. We even felt part of the forest, us with our voices, our bright colours and our noise. This was not a threatening forest, it was definitely friendly but demanding and getting our respect. Forest sounds surrounded us and we were always on the lookout for animals. We surely saw squirrels and the boys saw bears again, which no one else did. However, the best sight came when Wayne's leading pick-up jolted to a halt, throwing its occupants into a heap. There on the mountainside, an elk raised his head, stared at us for a while and then leisurely powered his way up the incline, disappearing into the trees. After that first marvelling thrill, we snatched up our cameras - all too late. The elk had gone and many hopeful pictures of the trees he was behind were taken - eat you heart out would-be wild life photographers!

The trucks trundled along the top of the mountain and here we could see the charred remains of last year's forest fires - the ones that had wrecked the basketball tournament and had seriously taxed the reservation firefighters. It is strange to be among these great flat-topped mountains. We have a mental image of mountains being sharp, jagged affairs, bare rock, topped with snow - like the Alps or the Himalayas. In this part of America the mountains are very old, their tops have been worn down by millions of years of erosion, vegetation grows there because of the warmth of the southerly latitudes. Through the thinning trees and from our vantage point, we could see the range after range of blue mountains stretching to the horizon, slashed by deep, indigo valleys. We would have long lingered there to drink in the majesty of this world and get some decent photographs, but Wayne was casting anxious glances at the clouds bubbling up and rushing towards us. When a flash of lightening flickered a little way off, he explained that the rainy season was beginning and we could expect sudden thunderstorms - the top of a mountain was not a good place to be!

Plans that the drivers had agreed were hurriedly changed; the trucks turned round, blankets were provided for those exposed to the elements and there began a ride that will outdo any other ride for the rest of our lives.

The trucks hurtled down the dusty tracks in breathtaking swoops; we hung on desperately as thunder rumbled around and the odd large drop of rain thudded upon us. We soon acclimatised to the motion and rode those bucking, plunging trucks like they were wild things. Was it scary? No, it was the most exhilarating, soul-stirring, intoxicating, hilarious trip imaginable. We laughed and joked as our bones were bounced hither and thither; clinging on like grim death we had a sensation like no other, a breathtaking thrill, shot through with laughter that just went on and on for ages. One of the funniest things was this. If you were in the following truck (and the lead changed from time to time...) you travelled through the dust of the lead vehicle and were thoroughly sandblasted. By the time we had returned to the car park at Cibecue, breathlessly falling out onto firm ground, not only had we been scoured and plastered with red sand, but our hair, also full of sand, stuck up stiff and straight and red, causing yet more gusts of helpless mirth. We were more red that Red Indians! There was time, however, to get cleaned up at St. Catherine's Mission and help Sr. Darlene with the preparation and loading up of the food for the Carrizo Pot Luck Supper.

The Carrizo Campsite is just off the highway and a few trucks had already arrived before us. The campfire was started and a convenient log dragged up for seating; food was unpacked and in no time the party was complete. We all had a go at making frybread; rolling the dough into a tennis ball size and flattening it between our palms, tossing it from one hand to the other until it is the size of a North Staffordshire Oatcake; then placing it on the wire tray over the campfire, turning it over as it quickly cooks into a substantial hunk of bread.

At this gathering, we were delighted to meet Rose and Juanita again. Rose had been the senior member of the Apache visitors to Staffordshire and everyone who met her had been impressed by her dignity. It was good to sit on camp chairs round the campfire; remembering their visit to us and passing round photographs of that momentous time. Undoubtedly, the star of gathering was one month old, Malik, Juanita's baby son, everyone held him for a few moments and voted him the most cuddliest of babies. He had unlimited attention when we were around.

In all our meetings with the Apache communities there were always many children around, children of all ages, shapes and sizes. One of the endearing sights was Fr. Bernard comforting a roaring three-year-old. Tears were streaming down his grubby face, he howled in misery while Fr. Bernard carefully and patiently removed the cactus spines from his face, hands and legs. He had fallen into a cactus patch. Whereas they were just typical children, getting into all kinds of mischief, laughing, squabbling, playing; there was not the same kind of frenzy we find at home of whining, demanding children and nagging parents. These children certainly thronged about and missed nothing, but they seemed so much more relaxed. Parents attended to their own concerns and allowed their children to play. A step too far out of line, however, brought a rebuke which was respected and heeded. For the whole of our visit we never heard a voice raised in anger in this intricately orderly, family society. The relationship between parents and children is one of mutual respect, although there must be some of the normal conflict between the generations - they stick together as families and their lives are centred on each other.

We were impressed to meet George, a frail and weathered elder who used to be a medicine man and his wife Ramona and their disabled grandson, Travis, at this shared supper. How we would have liked time to get to know him and hear of his life experiences.

It was at the Carrizo Pot Luck that we sampled an unusual pistachio salad that had whipped cream, marsh mallows, pistachios and other sweet things and was an extraordinary shade of green. It was very good, if you like very sweet things and was certainly something to experience.

Gradually the sun set and, as darkness rushed upon us, everyone packed up, collected children and slipped away home. This unexpectedly wonderful day drew to a close and as we sat outside our home in the warm evening, drinking Coke talking quietly, we agreed the whole day had been a lifetime's best.

The next day, Sunday, was our chance to add a little something to the everyday life of Whiteriver. The mission bell of St. Francis' rang out to summon the parish to Sunday Mass and the car park began to fill with cars. Wearing our official Exchange tee shirts, we sat together, near the piano while the church filled with families, both Apache and Anglo, who shot guarded, curious glances in our direction. The scent of incense - sacred smoke, billowed out from the sacristy and the measured beat of the drum signalled that Mass was about to begin. The drummer and an Apache parishioner bearing the bowl of sacred smoke led the procession, followed by Brother Ernie carrying the Word of God, then Fr. Ed, wearing his special Apache stole with tin jingles on the ends, and Fr. David in his own vestments. The drummer took his place with the rest of the musicians - two guitars, one of which was our Rachel and a little girl with shaker and tambourine. Fr. Ed added his guitar as the congregation sang the first hymn.

The sign of peace was exchanged and the sacred smoke was

offered to everyone to purify themselves. Then the Mass proceeded in the usual way; the readings of this, the seventeenth Sunday of the year, were very appropriate, as it happened, being about Elisha giving bread to the people and St. Paul's Letter to the Ephesians, saying there is one Body, one Lord, one faith, one baptism. The gospel of the day was the feeding of the five thousand, which fitted in with our singing of *"Bread of Life"* as the Communion hymn. Perhaps it was the emotion of the joining of so many diverse peoples together in one, familiar, unifying act of worship that added another dimension to the harmony of our voices and our singing was received so graciously. Fr. David read out a special message of friendship and blessing from the Archbishop of Birmingham and we presented Fr. Ed, Br. Ernie and Sr. Mary with official Apache Exchange tee shirts. Afterwards, many people came to thank us, ask about us and to enquire whether we were a touring choir - saying they wished they had recorded us! It gave us much pleasure to be so appreciated and feel that we too had something to offer.

Fr. Ed, Br. Ernie and Sr. Mary had invited us to an alfresco brunch at midday and at last Fr. Ed had the opportunity to sit down and talk with us.

He had been away the evening we had arrived, saying a Mass at a camp quite far away and then we had all been so busy in our different ways that we had never had the opportunity to get to know each other.

Fr. Ed has been in Whiteriver, for around ten years, ministering to his parish of some 225 scattered families. He said he does not feel so isolated now that Fr. Bernie is there, in Cibecue. Their parishes meet somewhere around the Whiteriver side of Cedar Creek. We asked about the other churches on the reservation. There seem to be many - Lutherans had been there first, but now there is a plethora of churches. Mostly they are Bible churches that seem to frown on ceremony and symbolism, relying on Bible study. This seems a difficult concept for a people unused to written language. All the churches had been sent to the reservation by the government as part of the settlement of Indian Affairs. But they do not seem to get on very well together. They were definitely against the Catholic Church, condemning the attendance of Christians and particularly priests at Apache ceremonies, speaking out against Fr. Ed at wakes and other situations where they come into contact and constantly complaining to the police that Fr. Ed heads a Satanist cult. His life in this regard is made difficult, veiled and actual threats appear regularly. The aim is always to discredit the Church by any means. Many attempts are made to try to get the churches to work together. The community tried to set up a panel of all the local ministers to help to tackle the big suicide problem, but of the 33 ministers in the community, only 9 turned up.

"It is so sad that they feel unable to join with us even on projects like this," Fr. Ed says. "But we must keep on trying. Our work, today, is Reverse Mission. In this we work with the people, bringing their philosophy, their ceremonies, their culture into ours, showing how we can all live together - rather than condemning all they do and trying to eliminate it. If I could not be involved in Apache ceremonies and spirituality, I would have to leave. If I came just to try and get people to become Catholics, I couldn't do that - it's against my nature and it is against what the Church is teaching today."

Reverse Mission recognises that, that we receive as well as give. We can see God in other places, in other lives. This does not diminish us. It simply opens our eyes, seeing a far bigger picture - far bigger than we could ever imagine. Long before Christianity appeared in this land, native peoples had their own way of communicating with God. They believe in one God who created all living things and who is concerned with the doings of all His creation. They have a tradition that Mary and Jesus were in this land, they even have a name for the Blessed Mother in the Apache language. So when the missionaries came, the story of the Incarnation was not strange to them. In their ancient culture, honouring the four sacred directions, marking themselves with sacred pollen in four places is the same action as making the sign of the cross. That must have startled the first missionaries!

Native Americans have always known how to pray and their

prayers are very powerful and meaningful and are not confined to simply asking for things or for help only in crisis. There is much meaning in their prayers; they understand blessing in a strong way. The sacred cattail pollen is used for many blessings - its colour is the colour of the sun, the colour of life, so it has a special meaning in so many situations. The Apache Crown Dancers bring blessings to the communities they dance for. When they dance, the Gaan, the Mountain Spirits, dwell within them and they are able to convey the blessings from these spirits. In their blessing, they pray that the people will use the power within them for good and in their dancing they re-enforce the message that ordinary people really do have the inborn ability to work for good.

The sacred smoke, made by burning dried sage and sweet grass, envelopes, blesses, purifies and strengthens, its gentle curling permeates the air, like spirits mingling. Fr. Ed often uses sacred smoke to help him focus his own spirit, its influence is not unlike incense and when he travels to Chapter Meetings of the Franciscans, he takes some sage and his guitar along with him.

One time when he did not have any sage, he asked the Tribal Chairman for permission to cut some. It is necessary to respect other peoples' ways, to tread carefully for fear of unwittingly offending. Oh yes, that would be OK. He was about to just go with his cutters to take a little, and then he thought he would ask Marilyn to go with him. They drove a little way outside Whiteriver, pulled over and walked to a patch of about twelve sage bushes. Marilyn looked at the bushes, carefully. "Let's see who is in charge here. This one I think," she said and going to it, she blessed it with cattail pollen and prayed for a while, asking permission of the sage bush to cut some. "Yes," she said to Fr. Ed. "You may cut some sage, just as much as you need, and no more." We would not think of doing that. We would just take what we wanted, maybe throw some away if we had too much. It is a whole different attitude, an attitude of respect.

I did remember though, that here, in England, if you need to cut Elder wood or pick Elderberries, you should ask permission of Mother Elder, explaining your need. No one else knew this. How far we have come away from these simple ways! We remembered the three fish-hooks at White Springs - gratitude for fish caught. Apache men still go hunting in the autumn, hunting together for large game as they have always done. When a deer is killed, it is laid down facing a special way; long prayers are said to thank the deer giving its life for the needs of the people - for food, for clothing and for the practical things each part is used for. No more is hunted than is necessary; the killing is as minimal as possible - definitely no massacre in the name of sport. All life is sacred and not to be taken away lightly - the effects of each action should be thought through and abandoned if it is wrong.

So the work of the Franciscans goes on with the Apache, they bring so much to the community and receive so much in return. In the Mass in which we had just participated, we had responded to the drum beat, announcing the arrival of the Word of God, listened to the prayers said in Apache and we had blessed ourselves with the sacred smoke, wafting it over ourselves with a fan of eagle feathers. And it just seemed so right. We could have listened to Fr. Ed for ever; he has such an engaging way of talking, so quiet, such conviction, so droll.

Can he speak Apache? It is a very difficult language to learn because it is not written conventionally and it helps if you can see the words as well as hear them, to be able to remember. The syllables of words are said very quickly and run together, so that you can't hear how they go. One word for God in Apache is "Bik'echo'ihi'dan" - "the one from whom all life comes". This word of four syllables sounds like one syllable. Then there are click sounds and minute pauses in sentences to complicate matters. However, we did manage to get a recording of the Lord's Prayer said in Apache and with a lot of effort have managed to write it down in our own sort of phonetics.

It was Fr. Ed who told us that the Sunrise Dance we should have attended had been called off. This does sometimes happen because it is very complicated to organise and very costly - so there had been a breakdown somewhere. Fr. Ed was going to teach us how to dance before we went to the ceremony so that we could join in. He said that the family of the Sunrise Girl lined up on one side and the family of her godparents line up opposite and they danced, to only the beat of the drum and the voices of the singers, towards each other and then back. You can't just get up and dance; you have to be asked. A couple, linking arms comes in front of you and dances on the spot, then as they dance backwards, you dance with them and are joined in the dance. "I was here seven years before anyone asked me to dance," laughed Fr. Ed. "I was dressed in my Franciscan habit - perhaps I scared them. Then at one dance three ladies came and danced to me. "Do you know, I have been here for seven years and this is the first time I have been asked to dance," I said to them.

"Well, sweetheart, it won't be the last," they said amid all the cheers and shouts. Both Fr. Ed and Fr. Bernard carry their roles as Catholic priests to the Apache with dignity and humour. By joining in with Apache life and Apache ceremony, they demonstrate their respect for the Apache and Native Americans - respect is something that has been and still is, sadly missing from the equation. Then Fr. Ed was called away on parish business and we felt privileged to have spent so long in conversation with him.

In the evening we headed for the restaurant down the road where we would meet up with Fr. Bernard and Sr. Darlene for yet another splendid meal. This was not just a restaurant, though, there were also high-class gifts on sale and we were able to purchase excellent White Mountain Apache jewellery and sweat shirts and tee shirts. Then back home again to pack a few essentials for our off-reservation excursion to the Grand Canyon.

On the road by 8.30am, we travelled north along the highway towards Hon Dah, Pinetop and Show Low, a road we now knew quite well. Those in the back of the minibus saw bears again. The trees do actually come right down to the road so it is not inconceivable that there could be bears. Apart from the power lines that follow the road, there is very little evidence of human activity - just a craft shop, filling station or small cafe here and there. However, as soon as you leave the reservation you are in the US, make no mistake! The long straight road is plastered with

Above: At last Fr. Ed had the chance to sit with us and talk
Below: We added the Nicoll family to our list of friends

advertisement hoardings and buildings of every sort, homes, businesses, offices, all hugging the roadside until they spread out into side roads and become small towns. The road signs are not foolproof, either, and coming to a road junction not experienced before, can become an exercise of trial and error. By the time we got to Taylor, there was a need for a comfort stop and happy chance we chose "Arby's". Our little needs tended and, for some, another breakfast, we returned to the car park. We were concerned to see water streaming from the engine of the minibus and dripping from somewhere at the back. What and why? And should we still continue into the unknown?

We were still pondering this problem, peering into the engine, when a station wagon drew up and Arby's owner Lynette Nicoll came to our aid. She looked into the engine, as mystified as us and rang her husband, Robert, who left what he was doing and came to help. Nothing was obviously wrong, but we all agreed it would be silly to go without finding out why so much water was still running out. With Robert's help we phoned the Hire Company and they immediately said they would send someone out to us and it would take about an hour. Robert had to leave but Lynette insisted that she would stay with us until we were on the road again. All this time, her three little boys, Aaron, Matthew and Joshua had been so good, waiting patiently. They played quietly with those of us not buried in the engine and in the long wait we got to know the Nicoll family and added them to the warm circle of friends we had made. Our meeting was so accidental and so brief and yet another important link in the great web of our humanity was forged. We now have someone else in Arizona to care about and keep in contact with. We already know that new baby Lyssa joined their family in November.

It was an enthusiastic air-conditioning system that caused our minibus problem and once checked out, we were on our way again. Funnily enough, after this, we saw many more vehicles with water running out of them; we had never noticed it before. We had lost two hours travelling time and had to rearrange our programme. We really had to be at the motel in Williams by 6 o'clock or we would lose our rooms and Fr. Bernard would lose the deposit he'd paid on them.

All the time on this long journey we played the Billy Ray Martin tape, *"Deadline For My Memories"*, over and over again, until we knew it so well it always says "Grand Canyon" to us whenever and wherever we hear it, just as Matt Redman's tape says "the road to Cibecue" to us, too.

At Holbrook we joined Route 66 and continued past Joseph City, Winslow, Winona, and Flagstaff and finally parked up outside the motel in the centre of Williams just before 6 o'clock. We had made it - and felt just a bit smug.

Rooms sorted and luggage stashed away, there was a short time for exploration before meeting up for the evening pizzas. This gave the leaders the opportunity to slip away and book the tickets for the train ride to the Grand Canyon next day before we, too, examined what Williams had to offer.

Williams is determined to preserve its reputation as a real Wild West town and, boasting a good selection of Frontier memorabilia and Indian craft shops and its adequate dining establishments, the whole is pulled together by the railway and the constant clanking, clanging railway sounds - both day and night. Everything seems to be geared to being on Route 66 and the tourist trade is paramount.

Our train journey was to be a surprise to the rest of the party and we had them down at the depot in good time for the 9am start.

Having been used to reservation life for a week, the crowds of people came as a bit of a shock. They thronged about the platform and outside on the street. Here two unsavoury western characters were harassing an innocent passer-by. Luckily the Marshall intervened and after a vicious gunfight they ran off, hurling threats. A country and western band serenaded us as we waited for the train to draw up. It was a real steam train, complete with cow-catcher, clanging bell and "Whoo-oo-whoo" just like the films and once on board, there was an car attendant to cater for our wants - snacks and Coca Cola in original bottles. A singing cowboy entertained us as the train chugged its way the 60 miles to the

Apache Exchange

Canyon. It took nearly two hours to get there and the passengers needed some entertainment, as there were many family parties on this Wild West excursion, the little ones dressed the part, complete with holsters and six guns.

I was feeling a little disappointed when the train drew in at the Grand Canyon depot. There were just so many people, thousands it seemed, pouring off the train to join the thousands already there. But then I was there, so why shouldn't they be too? I had been told to approach the rim with eyes closed and to open them to see only the Canyon - or just before you fall over the edge - a bit risky, I thought! Anyway, I kept my eyes firmly watching the ground and I looked...Wow!

I had seen the photographs, heard the broadcasts, watched the documentaries and knew what to expect. It was just like the pictures, but oh, so much more - as anyone will tell you who has been there themselves. Absolutely nothing can prepare you for the tremendous up-welling of emotion as you gaze at this scene. You know the Canyon is a mile deep and eight miles across in places and that, at the bottom, the Colorado River flows in its twisty course to empty itself into the Gulf of California. These facts are quite acceptable. However, this part of the river's journey is not just a gigantic slash in the earth's crust, more a ravaging clawing; a raking maul through the strata of millennia, a wound exposing the very skeleton of Earth, down to its creation. And we, insignificant specks in our daily thousands, can only stand and look, acknowledging our insignificance - and even only think in whispers.

The urge to get away from the crowds and find a quiet place where you could just "be", was very strong and we only had three hours before the train returned to Williams. We agreed to meet by the Hopi House in good time and then just split, seeking to wring as much as we could from the short time we had. Some went west along the Rim, some east and some down the bright Angel Trail, hoping to get as near the bottom as they could.

To get away from the clattering, chattering, camera clicking and whirring throng, to be where the tarmac was not, was the aim

The Grand Canyon

of the eastbound explorers. The tarmac path along the rim would serve to protect the rim from erosion by so many feet and who wouldn't be grateful for a seat or a meal or the toilet? These concessions to humanity were rather irritating so we set off at a brisk pace, in that hot temperature and thin air, to find our own special spot. After an hour-and-a-half we simply had to turn back, while the tarmac and the people still continued on out of sight. We found a quicker way to get back to our meeting place, but before we arrived, there was an ominous rumble of thunder and a few big drops of rain - and mysteriously all those noisy people disappeared! There was a deep silence and all that could be seen were the, now muted, colours of the Grand Canyon, the dark level horizon and the bubbling thunderclouds. So we spaced ourselves and sat on rocks to look and ponder our own mystical moment in what is, in anyone's culture, a sacred place. Maybe our minds and spirits were opened just a little more to God's ever present and deeper wisdom, giving us a tiny glimpse of how He works and that His ways are not our ways, His thoughts are not our thoughts.

The warm drops of rain were only few and the crowds soon reappeared - where they had been? But we had had our special moment and were satisfied. We had always known this trip would be the merest taste of the Grand Canyon and we would make the best of it, for the chance may never come again. We had done our share of playing the tourist, taking our photographs, watching the Navajo dancers, buying our souvenirs and have something precious to bring home besides. We can only hope that other people find the heartspace to see more than the view and to hear the sigh of eternity.

Back on the train, thunder rumbling, rain spotting down, we chugged our way back to Williams. This time, as we neared our journey's end, those vicious gunmen we had last seen at William's Depot, galloped up and held up the train in the best outlaw tradition - masks and all. They boarded it and demanded our money and jewels at gunpoint. We said we didn't have any so they moved on up the train, only to return shortly in the custody of the Marshall. We cheered. There were all sorts of diversions like this; mainly to keep the children amused on a long journey. What good children they were too, we were very impressed with the good behaviour of the American children. Without being repressed, they were obedient and respectful and in harmony with their attentive parents.

On the way there had been a heavy shower of hail that at first looked like snow and as we pulled into Williams there was an almighty rainstorm that sent us scurrying back to the motel. Our evening meal was at Denny's and as we ate, the rain stopped, the clouds cleared and the sun set in a blaze of glory that was breathtaking. As the rosy and golden sky colours changed and changed again against the retreating purple clouds, we could only watch, transfixed - for not a soul had brought a camera.

The gift shops of Williams were severely depleted, that evening, as we secured those goods we had already identified. We caused a bit of a stir ourselves with our English accents and all explained in many places just who we were and why we were there. Then we were on the road again, next day, to the sound of Billy Ray Martin, driving across Arizona to visit the Painted Desert and the Petrified Forest.

The land is flat but is also high desert, being of an elevation of about 6,000ft. It is the lack of a regular, appreciable rainfall that makes this a desert with its extremes of temperature and scrub vegetation. Route 66 cuts through this desert plateau country relentlessly to the horizon. Only in the far, far distance can the shadowy mountains be seen while the miles and miles of scrub grassland roll away in all directions. This had got to be one of the "lands where the buffalo roam" - there is so much space to roam. Along the roadside there is unbroken but unobtrusive fencing, which keeps the animals off the road and the occasional Indian Craft shop but little else. By the time we neared Joseph City, it was time for some lunch so we stopped at a crowded, roadside, filling station, choosing which style of cuisine we wanted - filling those empty spaces with burgers or salads or steaks. You can get some sense of how big America really is, how empty in some places, how teeming in others.

We knew what to expect at the Grand Canyon but were totally

Top: High Desert. Bottom: The Painted Desert

unprepared for the Painted Desert. This high dry tableland was once a vast floodplain, crossed by many streams and small rivers. Over the hundreds of millions of years, the land sank, was flooded and covered with layers of sediment washed out of the surrounding rocks. Then it was lifted far above sea level and the now layers of sedimentary rock were eroded by wind, water, frost and heat. The multicoloured strata of white, cream and yellow sandstone; grey clay darkened by a high carbon content; dark red iron-stained siltstone and lighter red iron oxide sandstone were exposed. All this gives a surreal desolate, abandoned landscape, which, at the same time is stunningly beautiful with its warm colours in neat stripes. We were lucky that it had rained, we were told, as the rain washes away the dust and makes the colours clearer. So it was still going on, even as we stood there looking over "the badlands", grain by grain, new landscapes are being created. At one point there was a path down, off the tarmac road, down to the actual desert. Naturally the boys plunged down, while we filmed them from above until they were merely colourful specks running up and down the multicoloured heaps of desert-sand. They said that the ground was all soft and sticky down there and was a lot hotter than it was where we were - and it was a long way back up again. We were grateful for this information and nourished them with drinks of water, secretly thankful we had resisted the temptation of running down with them.

    We progressed from viewpoint to viewpoint along the National Park roadway, taking in the sweeping vistas and stopping to read every available information notice. In all this beautiful desolation, humans had left their silent testimony in the ruins of their ancient stone houses and the messages they had left as petroglyphs - pictures pecked into the sandstone rocks. Although the interpretation of the messages is unsure, the number and diversity of pictures on one huge block - named Newspaper Rock, presents us with the notion of generations of time-forgotten people visiting this place to keep abreast of current affairs, adding their own contribution to the history.

    Next, there was the Petrified Forest. At the time of the dinosaurs,

Above: The Painted Desert 'badlands'
Below: ". . . just fallen off some gigantic logpile."

tall, stately pine-like trees grew along the banks of the streams and rivers that crossed this high tableland. These trees eventually fell and were washed along by the flooding waters onto the floodplain. Here they were covered with silt, mud and volcanic ash and their decay was slowed by the lack of oxygen. Water containing silica gradually seeped into the woody tissue of the logs and, over the thousands of years, the silica crystallised into quartz. The logs looked like wood, but their substance had been turned into stone. For 225 million years the land has sunk, been flooded, covered with more and more layers of sedimentary rock, been uplifted by volcanic action, stressed and cracked and worn away by wind and weather. As the covering rock, softer than the petrified wood, has worn away, these ancient logs are revealed, scattered over the ground as though they had just rolled off some gigantic logpile.

We wandered among them, touching; the eyes are so easily deceived but touch is not. The trail eventually ended at the souvenir shop where we spent a goodly time browsing through a welter of desirable mementoes. Somehow, nothing piled so high in enticing display did justice to what you could really feel in your bones and drink in with your eyes as you travelled through that National Park.

We were to meet Fr. Bernard and Sr. Darlene at Holbrook at 6 o'clock and we arrived with time to look round this old frontier town before our rendezvous at Butterfield's Stagecoach Restaurant. We did not know, at the time that Holbrook had played its own part in the history of the Apache.

When Geronimo and his few renegades surrendered, it had already been decided that the Chiricahuas and the Warm Springs Apaches should be transported the 2000 miles to Florida by train and it was at Holbrook that their train journey began. All the peaceful families of these two tribes, some 400 people, were rounded up and marched for six days the one hundred miles to Holbrook's railroad depot. They thought they were going to a new life, away from their hostile cousins on the reservation. They had all their belongings, their horses and their dogs and the night before departure, camped on the outskirts of the town. They drummed, danced and chanted round the campfires that night in anticipation of meeting the "Great Father" in Washington; only the dogs were uneasy, sensing disaster. In the morning they were packed into the eighteen tourist cars - doors and windows locked for the whole of their journey. Stops were made, but only at lonely water towers where food was put out in piles to be collected by one Apache for each car and taken inside. No one else was allowed to leave the car and, as the doors and windows were kept locked and there were no cooking or washing or sanitary facilities, the smell was overpowering in the September heat. Very few of the Apache had ever been on a train and never like this; their journey to prison in Florida was an appalling nightmare. All their belongings, their horses and dogs had had to be left behind. The goods and horses were sold, but the dogs, faithful to the end, ran beside the disappearing train, howling their despair and were shot by the soldiers and local cowboys. We did not know this gruesome tale as we strolled around this dusty, sleepy town and finally came together at Butterfield's.

John Butterfield had opened his overland route from St. Louis to San Francisco in 1858 to carry mail, but the service soon developed into passenger transport as more and more pioneers and missionaries travelled West. The relay stage at Holbrook was but one of the stopping places for an overnight stay, a meal or a change of horses. The restaurant today, maintains the nostalgia of those times with the really authentic looking decor that we recognise from films. Seated at the long table, with a good steak meal, you could easily imagine yourself back just over a hundred years. Would the conversation among the diners, centre on the spectacle of the defeated Indians, camping in their hundreds on the outskirts of the town?

Our excursion into tourist America was particularly good for us. We saw the awesome natural wonders; we met the ordinary people; we could see the desperate attempts to bolster, retain and exploit their history (while ignoring the thousands of years of history already in place in "their" land) and we acknowledged the undoubted success of American drive for commercial wealth. This was our world, a world with which we were very familiar - its loud voices, loud music, roaring traffic, insistent, intrusive advertisements, abundant food, overflowing commodities and the unending ringing of cash registers. Why, then, we wondered, as we drove into the reservation, plunging down the empty, silent road towards Whiteriver, were we overwhelmed by a quickening of the pulse and warm feeling of coming home? We were so homesick for Whiteriver, so homesick for Apacheland.

It came as a bit of a shock, as we made for our beds at 11.30, to find that two of the bedrooms were locked and the keys nowhere to be found. After all the recriminations, Rachel, Fran and Catherine T and Aidan and Steve were definitely bedless and in spite of all our earnest and cunning attempts to get their doors open, bedless they remained. Too tired to come up with any other solution, we made them beds on cushions on the floor and all slept the sleep of the exhausted. Sr. Mary made an early appearance the next morning and, with her master key, we quietly opened those stubborn doors (the keys were hanging on a hook on the inside) taking care not to disturb the sleepers. The mystery of how the bedrooms had been opened was strung out until midday to a battery of frustrated questions!

Fr. Ed was away from Whiteriver and Fr. David had agreed to say the Thursday Mass. Most of the Returners attended this Mass and, as we left the church, we were a little surprised to see we had visitors.

Since the visit of the Apache to England, we had known of 28 year-old Marianne who was so ill and in need of our prayers. We had always remembered her and sent her cheering cards and messages to let her know we cared. Now she had driven over with her mother, to meet us. Marianne is waiting for a kidney transplant. Both her kidneys failed 14 years ago and all this time she has battled with so many attempts at treatment. She needs self-dialysis four times a day and takes countless pills, waiting until her antibody count is low enough to make a transplant possible. The hospital on the reservation is entirely modern, having every facility and a highly trained staff, both Apache and Anglo, but still Marianne's antibodies are too high. She is able to get about, to drive her pick-up, to joke with Fr. Bernard and to look after her mother, all the time under the dragging shadow of illness - and Marianne's mother lives only to look after Marianne.

We were so pleased to meet them, at last and invited them to stay for lunch. It was lucky all round that Chris, the chef, was cook for the day. He produced a wonderful meal of omelettes and salad with a tomato sculptured into the shape of a rose, which he gave to Marianne's mother. Anyone who has made omelettes knows how difficult it is to have them hot for everyone at the same time - Chris made omelettes for 14 that day and we all sat down together. It really was excellent! Our Apache guests were very impressed with the boys doing the cooking and the girls clearing and washing up.

We had quite a relaxed day, that Thursday, just pottering about, rearranging our possessions after our trip, washing and ironing, visiting Basha's and the H-Mart for more family presents and the inevitable bucket of coke.

The two Catherines and Aidan spent all their spare moments, during our stay in Whiteriver, composing songs. They used the piano in the church, so if ever we needed them, that was always the first place to look. On that evening, they sang their songs for us - songs that reflected in words and melody all that we had come to understand about a people surviving in their ancient culture, in harmony with the Creator. We were very moved because the songs were so good, we had not known how talented our musicians were. They had even surprised themselves because inspiration flowed so easily in this quiet place. Now that the songs have been recorded with all the technical backing and arrangements, they can feel justly proud of their efforts while the rest of us simply bask in reflected glory.

Friday was a day for interviews. We had to do our share - after all, the Apaches in England had been perpetually bombarded with interviews, so we knew what was coming. In the morning, four of us each did a piece for the national Catholic Extension Magazine - on the phone to Chicago for nearly two hours. In the afternoon, Armadio, who had been in the England party and who was working for The Apache Scout came to do an article on us for this weekly newspaper. His brother, Frank, also from the exchange party, came too and, the interview done, we continued with friendly chat, remembering people and places and checking up on the accuracy of impressions on both sides of the Atlantic.

Fr. Bernard came to supper and confirmed the disappointing news that there had been a hitch in the invitation for us to attend a Sunrise Dance. This was something we had been looking forward to so eagerly, something we knew was very significant in our study of Apache culture. The family of the Sunrise Girl had called the whole thing off - which, we learned, was not unusual, these days. However, Fr. Bernard had fixed for us to be at the Food Exchange of another Sunrise Dance on the next day. We would not see the whole ceremony, which takes four days, but at least we would get a flavour of what it is all about.

We had more guests to this supper. Perry, the Navajo who had painted all the murals in St. Francis and St. Catherine's churches and his Apache wife, Hedy, dropped in for a chat. It was while we were sitting on the doorstep, deep in conversation, that we experienced something so eerie and so beautiful it took our breath away. We had got used to the season's pattern of clear sunny skies and summer heat, the bubbling up of clouds in the afternoon, temperatures dropping and cloudy evenings with heavy showers and sometimes thunder and lightning. On this particular evening, we thought nothing of the setting sun as it slipped down below Bear Mountain behind us but were startled to see a bright, golden shining on the mountain in front of us. We made a dash for our cameras and captured the spectacle while the glowing mountain tops threw back the sunlight into the darkening sky. As the glow faded and night took over, the velvet sky was filled with stars. We found again, the stars we have lost from our own skies, where the wasted light from our cities blots our their shining, leaving us poorer. Here in the soft evening, to the whirring of the cicadas, the sighing of the warm breeze, the gentle murmur of conversation, we sat under the bright star-web and we could have been any people in any time, any time since people first began.

The next day we were to plunge deeply into an aspect of Apache life which intrigued us and which was one of the compelling reasons for undertaking this cultural exchange - a Sunrise Dance at Whiteriver. The day to day harmonious, successful running of the community depends on the quality of the clan leader - qualities handed down through the female line. So the importance of women is never questioned, their status is assured, they have not needed to be "liberated". From the age of four or five, girls begin to learn the life skills needed by women for the proper running of her family and by the time she reaches puberty, her Sunrise Dance is her rite of passage into adulthood. The Sunrise Dance is a complicated, expensive, richly symbolic ceremony, involving a large number of people, blood relations and non-relations. The preparations for the ceremony are very important and need much care if things are to go well - goodwill is so essential to promote and maintain the cohesion of the whole community.

When a girl first menstruates, planning begins for her Sunrise Dance, but the initial step, nowadays, is to discover if she really wants this ancient tradition. Obviously, the "old" people want the old ways to continue, but the influence of modern culture gains in strength. Girls do have the final choice in this matter; some dismiss it as old fashioned but many do still hold on to this essentially eloquent ritual and gain much inner strength from it.

Once the decision is made, a date is set - usually in June, July or early August when the evenings and nights are warm and more family members are home on vacation. Then a site must be decided upon - it must be flat ground, near water, have plenty of wood available, be spacious enough for temporary dwellings to be built and have a large and suitable space for dancing. This could be the family's own camp ground or one negotiated with clan members or friends. The girl's father must engage a medicine man to conduct the ceremonies, taking him gifts of an eagle feather, turquoise, cattail pollen and his fee.

A very important decision is the choosing of the sponsor or "godmother". She must not belong to the girl's clan, nor to her father's clan, she must not be even distantly related. The godmother must be of spotless reputation; she must be strong, both physically and morally; she must be wise and know many things about life; she must be hardworking and not lazy, always setting a good example and she must be friendly and get along well with people. All these are qualities she will impart to the Sunrise Girl and a special relationship is formed that is binding for life, a relationship that is as demanding as one of kinship. Godmother is always there to advise, help and comfort; hers is the shoulder to cry on and, as she looks out for the girl's welfare and interest, her opinion is respected. Once the position of sponsor has been accepted, the sponsor and her husband and the girl and her parents call each other "My very good friend" - a bond that is outside the obligation to the clan and which serves to bind the Apache people even closer.

All these things settled, the building preparations begin for the ceremony. A big, shady arbour is made from long posts, cut from the nearby trees. The sides and top are made from brushwood, leafy branches and woven mats. This is where the food is prepared and eventually set out. Other smaller shades, a semi-permanent wickiup and other small shelters for food storage are built in the same way. This building is mostly done by male relatives or by unattached men who will be paid for their work and takes quite a long time, maybe a week or more. Sometimes the workers stay at the campsite and are fed by the Sunrise Girl's family; often they move to the godmother's camp and build shades there too, for the Food Exchange.

On the day before the actual Sunrise Dance, two important events take place. The male relatives of the Sunrise Girl and her sponsor attend a sweatlodge, where they prepare themselves, spiritually, for the ceremonies - chanting prayers to the pounding rhythm of the drums, the medicine man pouring water onto the hot rocks to create the scalding, purifying steam. At intervals they plunge into the cool waters of the nearby stream before returning to the sweatlodge to continue their suffering, offering it so that the Sunrise Girl might be blessed.

At this time, too, the medicine man makes the ritual paraphernalia that will be used - the decorated wooden staff, the drinking tub and the scratching stick. The staff or cane symbolises long life which is the most important quality bestowed by the Sunrise Dance; the girl will dance with it during the ceremony and perhaps will lean on it as a walking stick when she becomes an old woman. The straight piece of wood is stripped of its bark, and its end bent over to form a crook, secured by a rawhide thong. The medicine man paints the cane with a mixture of yellow ochre and water and, when this is dry, he ties two eagle feathers to the rawhide thong. One feather has a turquoise bead fastened to it and the other has two small, downy feathers from the gentle, friendly oriole bird. The eagle feathers symbolise protection from illness caused by evil powers and the oriole feathers are symbolic of a sweet disposition, an ability to get on with others.

Two more objects, made for the ceremony, are the drinking tube and the scratching stick. As physical beauty is important to any woman, anywhere, these symbols of how she should have care for her appearance work like this. Throughout the ceremony and the four days following, the girl must drink only through the 2 inch long, hollow, cattail plant stalk. She should scratch herself only with the pointed, decorated scratching stick. If she were to touch herself with her fingers or allow a container to touch her mouth, ugly sores - leaving scars, would appear on her face and facial hair around her mouth. These two she wears on a thong around her neck. Also round her neck she wears an abalone pendant which identifies her as White Shell Woman, another personification of Changing Woman. A white or grey eagle feather is worn in the hair, hanging down behind her - this symbolically predicts that she will live until her hair is the colour of the feather. The most spectacular is the beautifully decorated buckskin dress. It has small downy eagle feathers at the shoulders - enabling the girl to move as lightly as a feather. Then there is the large, tanned buckskin which symbolises plenty of meat - ensuring that she will never know hunger. A good supply of candy, cigarettes, chewing gum and fruit and plenty of sacred cattail pollen is also needed. So, what with the arrangements for the Sunrise Dance and the complicated and costly paraphernalia, not to mention the vast amount of food over several days, it is not surprising that a Sunrise ceremony is not taken on lightly.

All things are now ready, the men spiritually prepared, the dance ground arranged as it should be and families gathered together. Food for a large feast, donated by the godmother, is taken in procession from her camp to her protege's camp and welcomed with singing and dancing to the beat of the drum, which lasts well into the afternoon. In the evening, the Sunrise Girl is presented with all her ritual paraphernalia and is dressed in her sacred buckskin dress - which she will not wear again after her Sunrise Dance until she dies and is dressed again in it for her burial. Then follows more dancing and singing around the campfire until all the participants return for the night. The next day will start before sunrise and be long and exhausting but the Sunrise Girl prepares herself, alone in prayer, for her new role as a woman. In this prayer time, the Creator asks her the ancient question, the question that ensures a future for the People.

Shortly before sunrise a tarpaulin is laid on the ground at the centre of the camp site and up to twelve blankets are placed upon it, then a large buckskin is put on the top, its front pointing to the east. Around this pile of blankets are cardboard boxes containing sweets, chewing gum and fruit and two baskets, one of cigarettes and one of cattail pollen. The drum summons the people; they gather round while the Sunrise Girl, in her buckskin serape and carrying her cane takes her place on the buckskin, accompanied by an aunt, sister or girlfriend. The medicine man asks for the power of Changing Woman to travel on his chants and reside in the Sunrise Girl for the four days of the ceremony, so that during this time, she is prepared for the life of a valued woman.

Each of the eight stages of the ceremony is begun and ended by particular songs and there is usually a rest period between the stages. In the first, she dances alone on the buckskin while the drum beats out the chant which tells the Western Apache creation story and of Changing Woman, who, alone in the flooded world, sailed on an abalone shell and petitioned the Sun for a child. By the end of this dance, Changing Woman's power has entered her body and in the next phase, the Sunrise Girl, kneeling on the buckskin supported and instructed now by her godmother, re-enacts Changing Woman's union with the Sun which produced her son, Nayenezgene - Slayer of Monsters. He listened to his mother's teaching and advice and when he grew to manhood, he travelled far, putting things right and ridding the earth of evil.

During the third phase, the Sunrise Girl lies, prone, on the buckskin while her godmother massages her shoulders, arms, back and legs. She does this to mould the young body into the right shape so she grows up strong - her legs, so she can walk a long way and can stand for a long time without getting tired; her back, so that it will not bend over in old age; her arms and shoulders, so that she can carry heavy things for her camp and never get tired, always able and ready to help out whenever her relatives need her.

The cane is stuck into the ground, about 15 yards away to the east, for the fourth phase. The Sunrise Girl runs from the buckskin, around the cane and back. The cane is moved further away and she runs around it again. Twice more the cane is moved further each time. This signifies the four stages of life: childhood, adolescence, adulthood and old age and each time she runs the stage, the Sunrise Girl owns that stage, so owning old age ensures she will live until she is an old woman.

The next phase is also a running one, this time the cane is set out east, south, west and north and the running is to enable her to run fast for a long way, with plenty of stamina.

"Candy it is poured" is the sixth stage. The medicine man blesses the Sunrise Girl with sacred cattail pollen and pours candy, corn and coins over her head from a small basket. Because she is holy, everything in that basket is made holy and all the things in the other baskets and boxes are holy too. Her male relatives go among the crowd, carrying the boxes of goodies inviting people to help themselves. These holy things will be good to have.

When all this is finished, the crowd comes together again for "Blessing her". The Sunrise Girl and her godmother dance slowly and quietly on the buckskin while those who wish, line up to bless her with the holy pollen. They can ask the power of Changing Woman to grant them their petitions at this time.

The Sunrise Girl, her Godmother and her friend dance before the blankets and buckskin

Attended by the Crown Dancers, the Sunrise Girl is blessed with Sacred Pollen by the Medicine Man

The Medicine Man invites the gathered families to bless the Sunrise Girl and be blessed by her

Above: Sunrise Girl
Below: The Crown Dancers
© *Rico Leffanta, Courtesy of Smith-Southwestern Inc. Arizona*

The last part of the ceremony is "Throwing them off". The Sunrise Girl steps off the buckskin and picks it up, gives it a good shaking and throws it to the east, the blankets are shaken and thrown to the south, west and north. She does this so that she will always have blankets and shaking them means her camp will always be clean. Throwing the buckskin means that there will always be good deer meat in her camp and that they will not go hungry.

This ceremony has lasted about four hours and it is now very hot. Everyone goes to rest in the shade and have something to eat and drink. For four days after the Sunrise ceremony, Changing Woman's power remains in the Sunrise Girl and she is regarded as holy, able to bless and even cure. She has now passed from childhood and although she may only be 13 or so, she begins to grow in her status as a woman. Proudly she stands, beautiful in her youth and vigour, honoured by those who know her; she is treated as a child no longer.

These days are ones of family reunions and gatherings and the campground is well used. Sometimes the evening campfire is visited by the Gaan, the spirits of the mountain. These spirits enter the bodies of the Crown Dancers as they dance around the flickering fire to the compelling throb of the drum and bless all those present.

At the end of the four holy days, the girl's family prepare another great feast which they take in procession, with drumming, singing, chanting and joy to the camp of godmother. The bond between the two families is acknowledged and honoured.

This is a complicated and demanding ritual which, although it focuses on an adolescent girl, nevertheless has much to offer everyone there. It could not happen at all without the co-operation of a great number of people and serves to affirm their dependence on all members of the family and on friends who are not bound by blood ties. It reminds everyone, on a pretty regular basis, that the life-goals of health, prosperity and personal happiness are attainable and that the effort and sacrifice involved are a necessary part of life. Even more significantly, the very survival of the Apache depends on the younger generation. It is they who hold the future, but the older generation must pass on the time-tested ethic in a way that is accessible and timeless. The role of women in this orderly society is emphasised, for although they are responsible for most of the physically demanding and humdrum work of day to day living, their status is one of dignity and honour and is respected by the men.

Our own participation in a Sunrise Dance was limited to the first Food Exchange, as the next day we would be away to Cibecue for the last time.

"About 11. o'clock," we were told and duly presented ourselves at the godmother's camp - which was just off the road in Whiteriver. The camp was very quiet. Women sat under the shades or in the nearby wickiups, the younger women preparing food, the older ones advising or resting, children scampered about, old men sat and talked. Nothing much seemed to be happening and nobody rushed to us to explain anything. We felt rather awkward and hung around trying to look as if we should be there and wishing we had some peas to shell or some pot to stir.

Fr. David and I were "captured" by one of the gang of men who built the arbours and who were paid a few dollars which they spent on alcohol. Goodness knows where! He was drunk, even so early in the day, and he regaled us with his tale of horror. He had killed children, he said and old women, many of them. He went through the motions of machine-gunning them down. It was his own life or theirs, he said with tears running down his face and he wished he had not done it. He told us this story many times and, whether it was genuine remorse or the drink that was talking we will never know, he certainly was a pitiful sight and we were told, later that he had served in Vietnam. He was just another of its casualties.

Eventually we discovered that it would be more like 12.30 before the procession would be ready to move and decided that we would go home and come back later - we really felt in the way. A great debate followed as to whether we should go back at all, some wishing to forget the whole thing, feeling out of place, that we were intruding and, from the silence which greeted us, that we were unwelcome. Most of our party, though, thought we should go back and, even if the atmosphere was still so subdued, we should try to show that we were interested, that we respected the traditions and that we appreciated being there. They would be expecting us; we could not back out now.

Those who felt strongly stayed behind and the remaining eight decided to walk to the camp, as it was so near. There was more activity this time, more people, more noise and, yes, cheery waves to us. Pick-ups were being loaded with foil-wrapped packages, clingfilm covered dishes and brimming baskets, while human beings squeezed in wherever they could. Was it far to the Sunrise camp, we asked? No, about a mile up the road, was the reply. Although it was midday and hot, there was plenty of shade from the trees and, demonstrating that the English are not couch potatoes and we were pretty fit, we set off at a brisk pace, hoping it would not be all over by the time we arrived. However, we had only travelled a little way when Michael's, almost empty pick-up drew alongside and we were offered a lift. Being good at truck riding now, we hopped in gratefully and soon caught up with the rest of the procession.

All the vehicles stopped a short way from the campground and, continuing on foot and carrying all the food, everyone formed up behind the drummer and proceeded to the Sunrise camp, laughing, singing, calling and joking. We joined on at the end and danced into the camp with the rest. The food was placed on a long table at the side of the camp, under a shade; then we found an advantageous place to watch as the songs were sung, the prayers were said and the people danced to and fro. It was not long before Chris was asked to dance by some of the ladies. His height, his fair hair and white stetson immediately attracted attention and he danced every dance that day! Gradually all our party were dancing, what a good thing Fr. Ed had instructed us in the correct procedures. The dancing is not complicated and once you realised it was six steps forward and six steps backwards while circling to the left, the rhythm of the drum kept the dance going until the song had ended. There was a brief time for a rest while the medicine man spoke a long prayer and then the dance went on.

We were quite ready for something to eat when the drumming

eventually stopped and everyone lined up to help themselves from the long table. The covers were off and there was an amazing array of food. We humbly put ourselves at the end of the line; we did not want to intrude, but we did want to show that we really respected the tradition and appreciated their inviting us - also we were pretty hungry.

We were the centre of attention, however, for the children. They came to talk; to ask about us; to have rides and to tell us about themselves. I think the mothers were quite grateful that we entertained their children for so long. The feasting over, there were more songs and many people came to question us and to share an afternoon of pleasant conversations. Michael told us all about the Sunrise Ceremony and its significance, so we had first-hand information. The chance came to join in some discussion about the songs and we had a good look at the drums. They were "pot drums" of various sizes. A metal pot, like a deep saucepan without handles, has some water in the bottom. A skin is stretched tightly over the top, kept tight with a rawhide thong. The correct tension is maintained by keeping the skin wet. As the skin dries out, the drum is tipped to moisten it again. At last, we began to think we had better get back to the others at the Retreat Centre, as we had been away for such a long time.

Getting away was not so easy. We slowly edged towards the road, collecting our members and losing them again as someone else stopped for a talk. We were prepared to walk all the way back and had taken a few steps, when Michael's pick-up drew up beside us. We had a lift home. Actually we were pretty tired after all that dancing! We were so glad that we had been to that food exchange; after the uncertainty of the morning, we too could have been put off. We would have missed a rare experience. Although we missed the rest of the Sunrise Dance for that girl, we felt that we had put our bit in. She would certainly remember, for the rest of her life, that we had been there.

There was an evening Mass that Saturday at Whiteriver to which some of us went. Fr. Ed was away and Fr. John, the Dominican priest from Pinetop, said the Mass - so what with Dominicans, Franciscans and Salvatorians we were well and truly blessed!

The next day we had to be up early to arrive at Cibecue for the 10.30 Mass and some of our party were a bit under the weather after the food exchange feast of yesterday. We were in good time and positioning ourselves for a quick assembly into a choir, we watched as the little church filled with Apache families. Fr. David con-celebrated the Mass with Fr. Bernard and presented the Archbishop's greeting and blessing to the parish of St. Catherine's, Cibecue; Kath read the day's readings which were about the Children of Israel finding manna in the desert and St. Paul's letter saying that we must put on a new self that has been created in God's way. The gospel of the day was from St. John: "He who comes to me will never be hungry; he who believes in me will never thirst." Fr. Bernard's memorable sermon said that we are what we eat. If we eat good food, we look good. If we eat poor food, we soon look poor and have no strength. If we don't give our bodies any food we will die. Our spirit needs food too and we can nurture our spirit by giving it the food that Jesus gave us - Himself, the bread of life.

So once again our singing of *"Bread of Life"* fitted in with the day's liturgy and was much appreciated by the congregation, we had made our own contribution and were part of the family.

After the Mass, the families of Cibecue gathered together for a Pot Luck to wish us God Speed for our journey home. Slowly the meal came together in the community hall and was eaten amid friendly chatter - then the speeches. Fr. Bernard thanked us for coming and hoped we took a flavour of Apacheland home with us, even though our visit had been so short. We replied that, although we would be glad to be back home with our families again, part of our hearts would still be in the White Mountains with the Apache. We had not just had a good time; we had learned so much about the Apache and had come to know and love them. We felt so at home, so comfortable in their company, that they could be sure we would not only think of them constantly, but would take any opportunity to return. We sincerely hope that, now a link between the two cultures has been made, that they will be able to come back to us in England, perhaps even to further their education. Our doors are always open to them.

We had gifts to give; Fr. David had some vestments and articles for the new church at Cedar Creek; there were writings and recordings from three of our primary schools to the children of Cibecue and individual gifts. Fr. Bernard really appreciated a packet of Staffordshire oatcake mix, as that's one of the things he misses from his old life. Then the great farewell cake was cut. It was iced with roses and "Bon Voyage" - which took a bit of explaining. There was a rodeo in Cibecue later that afternoon which we thought might be fun. But although we waited for some time, nothing seemed to happen so we gave it up and slowly and sadly said goodbye to Cibecue. We invited Fr. Bernard and Sr. Darlene to supper the next evening, our last in Apacheland and with heavy hearts drove back over the mountain to Whiteriver.

The last morning saw us one more in Show Low, spending our remaining dollars on gifts and savouring this small town. I did hear that it is called Show Low because in the olden days two outlaw gangs laid claim to the area and eventually the gang leaders played poker for it. "Show high, I win. Show low, you win." Show Low won and that is how the little town got its name. The truth of this had not been verified! After a short stop for food at Pinetop, the straight American road, edged by its frenetic humanity, took us home to the reservation. The main activity of what was left of the day was packing, cleaning the Retreat centre and preparing a special supper for our guests later on.

In the late afternoon Armadio came to take some photographs to go with his article for the Apache Scout and, while we were posing, we discovered that Fr. Bernard and Sr. Darlene would not be the only visitors we would have that evening. So it turned out; quietly the car park filled up with vehicles and the Retreat Centre thronged with our dear Apache friends. They brought food with them to share and everything we had prepared too was put outside on the long table, speedily disappearing as the quiet conversations murmured and the children played. All this time the cleaning and packing was going on as well, for the Armstrong family were taking our luggage that evening to get it to the airport at Phoenix, leaving us with just our overnight essentials as hand luggage.

Then, suddenly we were called together and were presented with gifts - gifts so precious because they were real and unique and Apache. Six Camp Dresses had been secretly made for us while we were there and they were beautiful. We put them on immediately and promised to bring them with us when we return to Apacheland, so we can truly join in the social dancing round the campfires.

The boys had precious turquoise beaded medallions, which they put on and we were all given beadwork gifts. Armadio's family presented us all with Apache Great Seal tee shirts which were so very much appreciated and which can still be seen in Staffordshire at momentous gatherings, inviting interested enquiries.

Dressed, as we were, like the Apache themselves, blond hair contrasting with the black, we linked hands as a great prayer was said, first in Apache and then in English. A prayer of thanksgiving for our friendships; our love for each other in Christ; well wishing for our long and arduous journey to our homeland and hopes for our return. The whole concept of the Apache Exchange was deemed a success and blessed by the two priests.

The remains of the Farewell Feast were carefully packed and taken to needy families, nothing was wasted; then, true to the Apache way we had come to understand, they quietly melted away into the night.

It is not their way to make an exhibition of noisy goodbyes with waving hands and tears. But the heaviness of heart and sadness of goodbye is no less and we felt subdued, reluctant to leave; so sorry it was all over.

It was difficult to convince certain members of the group that they should attempt to get some rest before our departure at 4.30am and in the end we gave up trying. It was no problem, they said. They were quite used to staying up all night, they said and there were only a few hours before they would have to get up again. We would see how untired they were. We were not convinced, but wearily, we left them to it with strict instructions not to make a single speck on the newly spick and span Retreat Centre. We were all ready at the appointed time, locked the doors for the last time, piled into the minibus and, as silently as Apaches, left Whiteriver. The "night birds" had fallen asleep immediately, even before the minibus engine had been started!

The plan was to meet up with Fr. Bernard and Sr. Darlene at the junction of the highway with the road to Cibecue and for Fr. Bernard to take over the driving of the minibus to Phoenix Airport. We drove through the dark and somehow missed our rendezvous. Never mind, they were either ahead of us or behind us and we would all stop at Globe and effect the change over there.

Dawn broke, rosy and fiery, over Arizona as we sped on over its red earth, twisting round its grey canyons, off the reservation and down to its dry desert. The day was already hot when we sleepily disembarked for a comfort stop at a roadside cafe at Globe - where we had a good view of the road in all directions. Still there was no sign of Fr. Bernard and we began anxiously to calculate how much time we had to get to the airport. It was decided that, as both parties were aiming for the airport at a set time, we had better get ourselves there, hoping to meet up with them and our luggage. What a pity we had not taken more notice of the journey when we arrived. Still, we were pretty resourceful folk and set off towards Phoenix.

Following the little aeroplane sign, as you do when going to airports, it was not without a little consternation that our minibus gatecrashed Williams Gate Airforce Base! Aware that this is not on the tourist route, we did a neat, but swift inspection circuit and escaped without detection! It was only then that our confidence was a little shaken, especially when we realised that we could not remember what the airport was called. Time, by now was running out, but after a quick stop at a filling station, we were put on the right road for Sky Harbor and arrived, safe and sound at the feet of a very relieved Fr. Bernard and Sr. Darline with 15 minutes to spare. There was time for thanks and hugs and wishes of goodbye to them and the Armstrong family, who had brought our luggage, before we were whisked away through the formalities and were airbound for Chicago and Birmingham.

We saw the sun set over America and shortly afterwards saw it

The last sunset over America

rise again over the Atlantic - two sunrises and a sunset in one journey. Then we were back, struggling through Birmingham Airport with our bulging baggage, our cowboy hats, Rachel's life-sized cradleboard and the guitar, into the arms of our waiting expectant families - home again.

In Conclusion

We were quite prepared for the jet lag and we really were exhausted. It had definitely not been just a holiday and our exhaustion was mental and spiritual as well as physical. We were very unsettled, very unwilling to take up the strain of modern living. We longed to be back in the peace and tranquillity of Apacheland. One of the emotions we all felt was the inability to say how wonderful it had all been. We could present our gifts, show our photos and tell the anecdotes, but the deeper meaning of our experience was something we hugged to ourselves. We could acknowledge this secret feeling in each other when we met again; we just could not put it into words. However, the inevitable evaluation meeting had to be held and countless reports were written; our generous sponsors received their reports; radio interviews, and talks to local schools and societies were given. Gradually we began to order our thoughts and, as the days went by, we could more easily, recount our adventures.

We had travelled nearly half a world away and into another world. We had stepped backwards in time and had had a glimpse of the future. Our viewpoint was unique; a two year build up in our community - and not only confined to the ultimate participants; the stimulation of contact with real Apaches from the incoming leg of the Exchange and then the launching of our own twelve man mission for an intense contact of two short weeks. We learned much about ourselves, individually and collectively and were, unconsciously, able to set this knowledge beside the new concepts we were about to discover. Although we felt ourselves to be open-minded and very willing to learn, our minds were full of a jumble of preconceived ideas and attitudes that we were determined to put right. It is true to say we did not really have any idea what was in store for us, but at least we were nimbly able to re-order our ideas when the occasion arose.

For instance, our notion of Americans had been rather stereotypical. We discovered that they are not all rich, materialistic and insensitive as portrayed in films and TV. We found Arizonans to be very kind, generous, and helpful. There is still an air of the frontier about the place and definitely an atmosphere of "The Little House on the Prairie" - albeit further west. In the crowded superstore, in Show Low, a young man bumped quite hard into an elderly gentleman.

"Excuse me, sir," he apologised. "I wasn't looking where I was going."

"That's all right, son," the elderly man replied. "You just woke me up."

They parted, smiling. So polite, so courteous - so old-fashioned! We did not, however, see many, if any, African Americans or Hispanic Americans and we do know that Native Americans are ignored as though they are not there - and, when their presence is obvious, they are treated with suspicion and often contempt.

At the outset, the Apache in our heads were twentieth century world citizens, but in our hearts there was still a shiver of the nineteenth century. Even as we stepped into their land, we could appreciate the anxiety of those early settlers - we did not belong here any more than they did. The very first time the Returners went out alone into Whiteriver they experienced the true feelings of an ethnic minority. They felt out of place, vulnerable, under surveillance, different, inferior - until smiling the Apache faces and cheery waving hands of people who knew nothing of us, put them so much at their ease that they forget to be scared any more. We experienced no racism on the reservation - we were guests and friends.

There is a small buzz of confidence on the reservation. People have work to do; children have education to attend to; the reservation must be administered efficiently. But there is not enough work; more value and inevitably, more money must be put into education; the social and economic problems mount and multiply. Nothing is easy. So, although there are those who have grasped the chance to better their lives and on whose shoulders the future of the Apache nation will rest, there is so much poverty for the majority. Lack of employment, opportunity and motivation for a big proportion of the population - reckoned at 60%, results in despair. Acceleration is fast into casino gambling, drug and alcohol dependency and finally suicide. This shadow hangs ominously over the neat little houses, the satellite aerials, the up-to-date jeans and trainers, the pick-ups parked outside. No family is left untouched. Added to these problems is the perception, held by so many Americans, that the original inhabitants of the land are of no account; that they are second class people, to be despised and reviled. It had been the policy of the US government to educate the Native American away from the traditional ways. For many decades, right up to 1962, young children were forcibly taken away from their families and sent to boarding schools to be "Anglicised", made to conform to the American way of life. This was not successful, even from the American point of view. For the Native American it was very bad. Parents without their beloved children in the home forgot how to be parents. The sadness of a childless life made them doubt their own culture's ability to raise children and all the interaction of the extended family, so important in the development of confident young people, was lost. The long-term effect was profound. Many, swallowed up by the American culture linger in the oblivion of poverty or take on the lifestyle and values of their neighbours and are held up, derisively, as an example of all Native Americans. Although some Native Americans lead exemplary lives off the reservation and can justly take their place in that mixture of cultures as professional and commercial successes, the drive to be back with their families, back with the Tribe survives. The challenge is to maintain the old traditional values, the intrinsic nature of the culture, while taking their place in today's world. They cannot live as museum pieces. The reservations should not become historic theme parks; their people tied to old ways just for the sake of it. Our experience of life on the reservation shows that a balance between thousands of years of history and life in the twenty-first century can be achieved. It's not easy, there are many problems - some probably without solutions. Native Americans are as smart as anyone and they can be equal to anyone, even better than some. All they need is the chance to be believed in and to believe in themselves.

Many people understand that there is much more to the Native American than history will allow and that the world has much more to learn of their wisdom. They are not a backward people who must be cleared off the land in the name of progress - unfortunate but necessary. More people, possibly, are a little ashamed of the way it was done and is still being perpetrated. Consider this. For thousands of years America was isolated, while the peoples of Europe, Asia and Africa surged to and fro across each other's lands with waves of immigration, peoples displaced by wars and politics, stirring and mixing their cultures together, each culture seeking, one way or another, in its turn, to dominate and eliminate the others. Their aims moved from mere survival to self-aggrandisement, to wealth and power - revolutions in the name of progress bringing evils as well as benefits.

Time followed a different path in the Americas. Uninfluenced by other cultures, the ethic of Native Americans followed a purer simplicity, a harmony with Nature, a respect for the laws of the Creator. Is this true, today? Or do we romanticise the idea, fashion it whimsically to suit our theories of what is wrong with our world? We had to find the answer to this question.

The short answer is "yes" - it is true, even today. For those brought up on *"The Song of Hiawatha"* - yes, it is like that, still. It is in the air, all around. In the emptiness and the silences it is there; in the quiet way the Apache move through the land, leaving hardly a trace that they have passed by, it is there. It is a profound respect for all Creation. We do not own the earth; we share it with all sorts of creatures who have an equal right to their share. The earth sustains us and provides us with all we need; the earth is our Mother - to be treated with love and respect. All creation is our Brother, our Sister - we should live in harmony with them, neither misusing nor exploiting. Above all is our Father - the Great Spirit, the Creator, God. To Him we give respect and gratitude, we listen to His laws and strive to live by them. All people have a Path of Life to tread which leads to the Father when life ends. Each person must travel the Path alone - alone, but not unaided, for we live together with our fellows. Everyone has their own weaknesses to wrestle with, but must make their life-decisions with their ultimate destination in mind and take responsibility for those decisions. So a life of harmony is the aim, with consideration for each individual and their personal life-space; for the land, the very rocks, trees and streams; for the greatest and the most minute of living things. Respect is given to the older generations, their opinions are sought and given weight, they are vital members of society, valued for the wisdom of experience they contribute. Value is also put upon children. They are welcomed, nurtured and reared with care to carry on the ancient lifestyle of their ancestors. The importance and acceptance of each person in the family is significant, for each individual is responsible for the whole group and the whole group is responsible for each individual. No one is left outside. Underpinning the intricate social structure is the awareness of the spirit of God throughout their lives and through the whole creation.

The Apache worship One God and see His spirit in all that is around them. So they acknowledge God's presence in the physical features of the land - His spirit is the Spirit of the Mountains; they see the presence of His spirit in the life-giving waters, His spirit in the air we breath, His spirit rests in the sacred places. Animals too have God's spirit in them and have their place along with human beings in the plan of creation. The beauty of creation is everywhere and each beautiful thing sings unending praise to the Creator, each obstacle in life is a test of faith in the unquestionable love of the Creator and the purpose of each life is to honour the design of creation with respect and reverence.

We thought this ideal life might have disappeared, if not under the rigours of persecution, certainly under the influence of TV. There are at least as many rogues, scoundrels and inadequates here as in any society; there must be criminal organisations to service the drugs and gambling; it would be naive to think otherwise - even Apaches are only human. We did not encounter the downside of life on the reservation everyone we met showed us how they were striving to live the best of lives. Most of our acquaintances are Christians and this alone brought us together. We are all equal, we share a universal Faith and we were as at home at an Apache Mass as we would be in our English parishes - we spoke the same language.

This is what we ordinary Staffordshire folk found in that beautiful, remote, unspoilt land so far away - the presence of God's Spirit everywhere, in spite of modern ways. Perhaps from our own standpoint of active Christianity, we were more aware of this. We very ordinary folk, with no special qualifications and only a short time for investigation found a common thread of humanity among a forgotten, disregarded people. Doubtless we missed many aspects of Apache life, but we brought home a race memory that has been forgotten for centuries in the developed world. This is the acknowledgement that the presence of God's Spirit is right here too, here in the beauty of our own land and our own peoples no less than in Apacheland. What we lack, what we have forgotten, what has so small a place in our economy is respect for the value and dignity of each and every morsel of creation. Mankind does not own the earth and all that is in it, however clever we think we are. Looking round at all our worldwide misuse, exploitation, pollution and devastation of lands and peoples - who really are the ignorant savages?

It takes a culture shock like the Apache Exchange to see the whole picture; a picture that reaches right around the world we know and also the world's other unconsidered places. Then can we understand the revelation that we are all only people - multitudinous and very diverse; that we are all brothers and sisters, all sharing the same planet and are all the children of one God - Creator - Great Spirit - Usen.